T. V. Kattimani

Hunters and the Holy Man

A Saga of the Bedagampana Tribe

PETER LANG

Chennai · Berlin · Bruxelles · Lausanne · New York · Oxford

Bibliographic information published by the Deutsche Nationalbibliothek. The German National Library lists this publication in the German National Bibliography; detailed bibliographic data is available on the Internet at http:// dnb.d nb.de.

A catalogue record for this book is available from the British Library.

Library of Congress Cataloging-in-Publication Data
A CIP catalog record for this book has been applied for at the Library of Congress.

© Cover image: Mayank Singh Shyam

Contact No - (+91)7000534256
Cover design by Peter Lang Group AG

ISBN 978-1-80374-879-5 (print)
ISBN 978-1-80374-880-1 (ePDF)
ISBN 978-1-80374-881-8 (ePub)

DOI 10.3726/b22522

© 2024 Peter Lang Group AG, Lausanne
Published by Peter Lang Pvt Ltd, Chennai
info@peterlang.com – www.peterlang.com

T.V. Kattimani has asserted his right under the Copyright, Designs and Patents Act, 1988, to be identified as Author of this Work.

All rights reserved.
All parts of this publication are protected by copyright.
Any utilisation outside the strict limits of the copyright law, without the permission of the publisher, is forbidden and liable to prosecution.
This applies in particular to reproductions, translations, microfilming, and storage and processing in electronic retrieval systems.

This publication has been peer reviewed.

Contents

Preface ... vii

Chapter 1 Discovering Bedagampana ... 1
Chapter 2 Origin, History, and Oralities ... 11
Chapter 3 Socio-Economic Conditions and Dietary Practices ... 25
Chapter 4 Cultural Practices and Beliefs ... 35
Chapter 5 Education, Health, and Infrastructure ... 55

Epilogue Vegetarianism and Assertion for Scheduled Tribe Inclusion ... 81

Bibliography ... 91
Index ... 95

Preface

As we move ahead to a world of digitalization and globalization, on the threshold we leave behind many things. It includes our lifestyle, values, societal norms, culture and even our people. Sometimes due to our internal choices, we adopt a different pathway whereas many times external forces push us away towards a cultural change. The book *Hunters and the Holy Man: A Saga of Bedagampana Tribe* is a narrative of resilient legacy of a tribal group called Bedagampana who over the period of time has loosen their tribal identity due to both internal choices of leaving their primary lifestyle of being hunters and adopting vegetarianism and external elements like cultural assimilation. This tribal society is still in transition where in some aspects of life they have continued their tribal attributes like nature worshipping, a female-oriented society whereas in some other domains, they are now homogenized with their neighboring community of 'Veerashaiva'.

One of the fundamental factors that has led to their identity loss is the lack of documentation. If we inquire into the existing review of literatures, we find that their existence is comparatively negligible. Hence, this book is an attempt to document their existence, their lifestyle, their way of sustainability and peaceful coexistence with nature, their wandering voices and their persistent struggle for insertion in the Scheduled Tribe category.

This is a story of a hunting tribe who over the period of time became vegetarian. It is a chronicle of indigenous people who exist on ground but are nowhere to be found on the white pages. Similarly, it is a tale of a society who inhabit in dark without electricity, water or road facilities in the mid of a jungle. The work endeavors to bring out the complex threads of their lives to the mainstream world. As they continue to fight for their land, rights and their belongingness, the work is an attempt to preserve their vulnerable identities and culture, give their silenced whispers a voice and rectify the historical injustices.

In this journey of writing this book I would like to thank Shanta Mallikarjuna Swami, the Head Seer of Salur Mutt, Puttanna, a local Bedagampana

PREFACE

community leader, K.V. Mahadev, a Bedagampana community priest cum leader for Bedagampana rights, Madaiah, a school teacher, an tribal healer Puttanna and Suresh, a retired teacher of school run by Salur Mutt for their assistance in discovering the past and present of Bedagampana tribe and their demands for a promising future.

I extend my profound wishes to Dr. Nagesh M., Assistant Professor, Department of Social Work, Central Tribal University of Andhra Pradesh, Dr. Debanjana Nag, Faculty Member, Central Tribal University of Andhra Pradesh and Vageesh Kumar Mishra, Research Assistant, Govind Ballabh Pant Social Science Institute, Prayagraj for their contribution in completion of this project.

My profound thanks to Dr. Vaddagere Nagarajaiah, a poet, social activist, and researcher who has helped the work in bringing the cultural and historical background of the Male Mahadeshwara and Bedagampana tribe. His scholarly suggestions based on his field experience have enriched the book.

My heartfelt thanks to Mayank Singh Shyam, a widely acclaimed Gond tribal painter of Patangadh, Madhya Pradesh for his generosity to accord his permission to use his valuable painting as the cover page of the book. He has a great tradition of painting. His father Late Jangarh Singh Shyam, popularized the Gond tribal painting, and his mother Nankusia Bai, is a legendary painter of contemporary time.

Since the beginning, it was my intent to make the book available not only for Indian society but also for the International audiences so that they can get a glimpse of the vulnerable indigenous cultures and the need for their preservation. In this regard, I thank Indrani Dutta, Acquisitions Editor, Peter Lang Group, and their entire team for acceptance of the proposal and their quick moves for the publication of the book.

Hope the book will be a guide for many interested scholars working in the field.

T.V. Kattimani

CHAPTER 1

Discovering Bedagampana

The Bedagampana, a tribe living in the heart of Male Mahadeshwara Hills of Hanur taluka of Chamrajnagar district of Karnataka is a lesser known yet culturally rich community. It is characterized by its unique socio-cultural aspects that set it apart from other tribal groups of India. One of the most distinctive features of the Bedagampana is their predominantly vegetarian diet, which is unusual among the tribal groups known for their reliance on hunting and gathering. This dietary preference is deeply rooted in their cultural and religious beliefs, reflecting a lifestyle that is both harmonious with nature and spiritually significant. The Bedagampanas' adherence to vegetarianism not only influences their daily lives but also plays a crucial role in their social identity, distinguishing them from other indigenous communities.

One of the most compelling aspects of the Bedagampanas' lifestyle is their deep connection to the hills. The tribe's settlements are often found in hilly regions, where they have adapted to the challenging terrain and developed a sustainable way of living. This connection to the hills is not merely geographical but also cultural and spiritual. The natural environment plays a crucial role in their daily lives, influencing their agricultural practices, dietary habits, and even religious beliefs. The hills are seen as sacred, and the Bedagampanas' reverence for nature is evident in their rituals and ceremonies, which often involve offerings and prayers to deities believed to reside in the hills.

The unique socio-cultural identity of the Bedagampanas, combined with their historical merger with the Veerashaiva and Lingayats and their enduring connection to the hills, underscores their assertion for inclusion in the Scheduled Tribes list. The tribe's integration with the Veerashaiva and Lingayat community is a significant socio-cultural phenomenon. The Veerashaiva and Lingayats are a prominent religious community in southern India, known for their worship of Shiva and adherence to specific rituals and practices. According to Hunsal (2004),

CHAPTER 1

> The Lingayat monotheistic movement was led by the non-priestly oppressed masses of India. Hence it could revolutionize life and society in all its aspects.

The major theology of Lingayatism was based on avoiding anger, ego, desire, and hatred, celibate atma (soul), and brahman (universe), submission to spirituality (bhakti), compassion, faith, moksha (salvation), chanting, worship, belief in doctrines and dogma (idea or opinion), philosophy, truth, honesty, humility, kindness, meditation, mind, concept of soul (Munavalli, 2007) which were easy for the common deprived people to understand and follow. It did not require any extravagant ceremony but was simplistic which connected simple hilly Bedagampana tribal people to be connected with this ideology. The Bedagampanas' merger with the Veerashaiva and Lingayats can be attributed to various socio-cultural practices and historical interactions. Despite this integration, the Bedagampanas have managed to preserve their unique cultural identity. Their traditional customs, rituals, and way of life continue to reflect their distinct heritage, even as they participate in the broader practices of the Lingayat community.

The assimilation of the Bedagampana tribal community with the Veerashaiva and Lingayats is a testament to the transformative power of religious movements in fostering socio-cultural integration and addressing social inequalities. The Lingayat movement, initiated by Basaveshwara in the 12th century, emerged as a progressive force that resonated deeply with oppressed masses, including the Bedagampana. This integration was facilitated by a combination of theological appeal, socio-economic factors, cultural exchange, historical interactions, and geographical considerations.

The Lingayat movement's core theological principles like a religion free of caste, creed, race, and gender, revolved around the simplicity of rituals and accessibility to all, which played a crucial role in attracting the Bedagampanas. The movement emphasized avoiding anger, ego, desire, and hatred while promoting celibacy, spirituality (bhakti), compassion, faith, and moksha (salvation). Unlike the elaborate rituals and ceremonies of Brahminical Hinduism, Lingayatism offered a straightforward spiritual framework that the deprived and marginalized sections of society could easily comprehend and practice.

For the Bedagampana, a tribal community with their own spiritual beliefs and practices, the Lingayat principles of truth, honesty, humility, kindness, and the concept of the soul (atma) were particularly appealing. The simplicity of Lingayat worship, devoid of extravagant ceremonies, resonated with the Bedagampanas, who were accustomed to a more direct and personal spiritual experience. The chanting, worship, and meditation practices of Lingayatism were compatible with the existing spiritual traditions of the Bedagampanas, facilitating their integration into the broader Lingayat community.

The socio-economic conditions of medieval India also played a significant role in the assimilation of the Bedagampanas with the Veerashaiva and Lingayats. As a marginalized tribal community, the Bedagampanas faced social exclusion and economic hardships due to their geographical isolation. The arrival of the Lingayat community provided a new socio-economic framework for the Bedagampanas. The inclusive nature of Lingayatism, which welcomed all individuals regardless of their caste or social status, facilitated the integration of the Bedagampanas into the Veerashaiva and Lingayat communities.

Despite their assimilation into the Veerashaiva and Lingayat fold, the Bedagampanas managed to preserve their unique cultural identity. This preservation was enabled by the inclusive and adaptive nature of Lingayatism, which allowed for the coexistence of diverse cultural practices within its broad framework. The traditional customs, rituals, and way of life of the Bedagampanas continued to reflect their distinct heritage, even as they participated in the broader practices of the Veerashaiva and Lingayat communities.

The cultural exchange between the Bedagampana , the Veerashaiva, and the Lingayats were mutually enriching. While the Bedagampanas adopted the theological and social principles of Lingayatism, they also contributed their own cultural elements to the Lingayat tradition. This syncretic process added new dimensions to the cultural and spiritual practices of the Lingayat community. The Bedagampanas' music, dance, and folk traditions found expression in Lingayat festivals and rituals, creating a vibrant and diverse cultural landscape.

Historical interactions and political dynamics also influenced the assimilation of the Bedagampanas with the Veerashaiva and Lingayats. During the medieval period, the rise of regional kingdoms and the spread of various religious movements shaped the socio-political landscape of the Deccan region. The Lingayat movement, with its strong social and political ethos, played a crucial role in these developments. The Bedagampanas, who inhabited the hilly and forested regions, had historical interactions with Lingayat communities through exchanges. The political support and patronage of Lingayat facilitated the assimilation process. The establishment of Lingayat mutts (monastic centres) and the patronage of Lingayat saints and scholars provided a socio-political framework that encouraged the integration of marginalized communities like the Bedagampanas.

Geographical factors also played a significant role in the assimilation of the Bedagampanas with the Veerashaiva and Lingayats. The hilly region of Male Mahadeshwara, where the Bedagampanas traditionally resided, presented challenges for the Lingayats, who found it difficult to survive in such a rugged and inhospitable terrain. The Bedagampanas, having lived in this region for generations, had developed the skills and knowledge necessary to thrive in this rough environment. The Lingayats' assimilation of the Bedagampanas can thus be seen as a strategic move to ensure a better and easier livelihood. By integrating with the Bedagampanas, the Lingayats gained access to the local knowledge and expertise needed to navigate and survive in the challenging terrain of Male Mahadeshwara Hills. This geographical convergence created a symbiotic relationship between the two communities, fostering socio-cultural integration while allowing the Bedagampanas to preserve their unique cultural identity.

The assimilation of the Bedagampanas with the Veerashaiva and Lingayats represents a significant chapter in the socio-cultural history of the Male Mahadeshwara Hills. The theological appeal of Lingayatism, its simplistic and egalitarian practices, and its strong stance against caste discrimination provided compelling reasons for the Bedagampanas to join the Veerashaiva and Lingayat fold. Socio-economic aspects, cultural exchange, historical interactions, and geographical considerations further facilitated this integration.

Initially, the assimilation into the Lingayat fold offered the Bedagampanas a respite from socio-economic hardships. The egalitarian and inclusive principles of Lingayatism, with its emphasis on simplicity and accessibility, resonated deeply with the Bedagampanas, who found in it a spiritual and social framework that provided dignity and a sense of belonging. However, as the Lingayat community grew and evolved, the cultural and social practices of the Bedagampanas began to be overshadowed by the dominant Lingayat norms and traditions.

One of the primary factors contributing to the identity crisis was the gradual erosion of the Bedagampanas' unique cultural practices. While the initial integration allowed for a syncretic blending of traditions, over time, the dominant Lingayat culture began to subsume the distinct customs, rituals, and traditions of the Bedagampanas. The rituals, folklore, and tribal customs that were integral to Bedagampana identity slowly lost prominence as the community adapted to the broader Lingayat practices.

Moreover, the socio-political dynamics of the region further exacerbated the identity crisis. As the Lingayat community gained prominence and political power, the socio-political identity of the Bedagampanas became increasingly conflated with that of the Lingayats. This conflation often meant that the specific needs, concerns, and issues of the Bedagampana people were overlooked or marginalized in favour of the broader interests of the Veerashaiva and Lingayat communities. The political representation and social recognition that the Bedagampanas initially hoped to gain through integration began to fade, leaving them feeling alienated and underrepresented within the larger Veerashaiva and Lingayat framework.

Additionally, the geographical and economic factors that initially facilitated the integration also played a role in the identity crisis. The Bedagampanas, who were adept at surviving in the challenging terrain of Male Mahadeshwara, initially provided valuable knowledge and skills to the Lingayat community. However, as economic conditions and livelihoods changed, and as the region became more accessible and integrated into broader economic networks, the traditional knowledge and skills of the Bedagampanas lost their relevance. This economic marginalization further contributed to their sense of disenfranchisement and identity loss.

For decades, they have been fighting for their rights to be included in the Scheduled Tribe list of the Government of India. This inclusion is not merely a matter of administrative classification but a recognition of their distinct cultural heritage and the challenges they face. Being included in the Scheduled Tribes list would provide the Bedagampana with certain legal protections and access to various government benefits aimed at improving the socio-economic conditions of Bedagampana indigenous people. The process of asserting their inclusion in the Scheduled Tribes list involves highlighting the distinctiveness of their cultural practices, the socio-economic challenges they face, and their historical roots. It is a way for the Bedagampanas to seek recognition and support for preserving their unique way of life while also addressing contemporary issues such as access to education, healthcare, and economic opportunities. This inclusion would help safeguard their cultural heritage and ensure that the benefits of development reach their community.

> The Bedagampana community, with its roots tracing back over 600 years, holds a significant historical and cultural legacy. Originally, from Srikalahasti, Andhra Pradesh, they migrated to the high hills of Bargur, Kadambur, and Talavadi, along with areas in Karnataka, due to a monarch's demand for a spouse from their community. Today, they inhabit regions across Karnataka and Tamil Nadu, including Male Mahadeshwar Hills, Kollegala, and Hanur Taluk, where they engage in agriculture, cattle and sheep rearing (The Hindu, April 5, 2021).

The Bedagampana's agricultural practices are a testament to their adaptability. Engaging primarily in subsistence farming, they cultivate crops suited to the hilly terrain and local climate, which include millets, pulses, and vegetables. This farming is often complemented by cattle and sheep rearing, providing them with dairy products. These activities are deeply interwoven with their cultural identity and social structure, with agricultural cycles and livestock management being central to their community life and festivals. Despite their historical significance, the Bedagampana community remains relatively undocumented.

With a population of approximately 31,500 in specific regions and 19,240 in Karnataka alone, there is a growing need for comprehensive documentation and understanding of their culture and practices (Jyothi H. P., 2020).

Recent studies highlight the intricate relationship between the Bedagampana tribe and the local ecosystem. Puttahariyappa et al. (2021) shed light on:

> their utilization of wild plant species for sustenance, traditional medicine, and cultural identity. With 124 species from 57 families and 91 genera identified, these plants play a crucial role in their dietary habits and economic well-being, contributing up to 15-20% of their household income.

Understanding the indigenous healing practices and dietary traditions of the Bedagampana community is essential not only for preserving their cultural heritage but also for improving their socio-economic conditions. The use of wild plants by the Bedagampana community not only underscores their profound knowledge of local biodiversity but also underscores their sustainable practices that have enabled their resilience over centuries. These plants are not merely sources of food and medicine but are integral to their cultural rituals and daily life, reflecting a holistic approach to health and well-being rooted in their indigenous knowledge systems. Proper documentation and research can help in recognizing their contributions to biodiversity conservation and sustainable livelihoods.

The work aims to delve into the socio-cultural and economic landscape of the Bedagampana community residing in Male Mahadeshwar Hills, Karnataka. The Bedagampana tribe, like many other tribal communities in India, faces challenges such as poverty, health, education, drinking water, inequality, and marginalization. This study seeks to understand and describe their socio-cultural, educational, and economic status, including their indigenous knowledge systems related to dietary, health, nutritional, and healing practices. The research also tries to find out the existing oralities and also to explore uncovered issues like gender, child marriage, geriatric problems, and other less focused issues. This will help the readers to understand the socio-cultural characteristics of the Bedagampana Tribal group, the religious practices observed within the community, the status of women and prevalence of child marriage in Bedagampana society, their agricultural and hilly lifestyle contributing to their income generation, and so on. Being a hilly tribe, the primary occupation should have been hunting and gathering, but what circumstances led them to remain a vegetarian tribe, and from when? Whether to remain vegetarian is an internal choice or an external force? All these questions are very important to understand the Bedagampana tribe.

India has specific laws and policies aimed at protecting the rights and cultural heritage of indigenous peoples. These may include recognition of indigenous land rights, provisions for cultural preservation, and support for indigenous languages and traditions. However, various news reports suggest the problems of relocation, identity loss, etc. in regard to the Bedagampana tribal community. The national governments actively support efforts to preserve and promote tribal culture through funding, capacity-building initiatives, and collaboration with indigenous communities.

However, despite legal protections and government support, indigenous cultures like Bedagampana face numerous challenges at the national level. These may include encroachment on indigenous lands, lack of access to education and healthcare, discrimination, and marginalization. Tribes like Bedagampana are engaged in efforts to revitalize and reclaim their cultural traditions at the national level. This may include language revitalization programs, cultural festivals, traditional arts and crafts initiatives, and community-based education initiatives. Indigenous rights movements play a crucial role in advocating for the rights and cultural preservation of Indigenous peoples at the national level. Various movements have been led by Bedagampana community leaders already to raise awareness, lobby for policy changes, and empower the aforesaid population to assert their rights. These initiatives are essential for ensuring that cultural preservation efforts are rooted in the needs and priorities of indigenous peoples. Apart from this, it is important to empower women through education, leadership opportunities, and access to resources are essential for the long-term sustainability of the Bedagampana community.

The tribal status of the theme area focusing on the Bedagampana is very crucial. Empowering tribal cultures through education, leadership opportunities, and access to resources is essential for the long-term sustainability of indigenous cultures. Bedagampana who already has become a sandwich culture between the Veerashaiva and Lingayats, their tribal cultural elements need proper policymaking for their development. By working together and prioritizing the rights and voices of Indigenous peoples, we can ensure that Indigenous cultures continue to thrive. Further, by implementing inclusive policies and initiatives, we can ensure that the cultural heritages of such vulnerable communities can endure for future generations. Through these concerted efforts, one can uphold the dignity and rights of indigenous peoples while highlighting their rich heritages and cultural landscape as a soft power of the country at a global level. Hence, the book is based on the following research hypothesis:

- The Bedagampana tribe exhibits unique socio-cultural aspects.
- Bedagampana might be distinct in consuming predominantly vegetarian diets compared to other tribes.

CHAPTER 1

- The Bedagampanas are primarily a tribe and due to various socio-cultural practices, they are compelled to merge with the Veerashaiva and Lingayat communities.
- Due to their lifestyle and connection to the hills, Bedagampana may assert their inclusion in the Scheduled Tribes list.

The Bedagampana tribe, with its unique socio-cultural aspects, predominantly vegetarian diet, historical homogenization with the Veerashaiva and Lingayat communities, and deep connection to the hills, stands as a testament to the rich diversity of indigenous cultures in India. Their assertion for inclusion in the Scheduled Tribes list is a significant step towards recognizing and preserving their distinct identity while addressing the socio-economic challenges they face. The Bedagampanas' journey is one of resilience and adaptation, reflecting the broader narrative of Indigenous communities striving to maintain their heritage and preserve their identities in a rapidly changing world.

The chapters ahead will try to understand the educational status of the Bedagampanas, their dietary practices, their economic and livelihood aspects, the division of labor in the society, their religious practices, their indigenous knowledge systems, including tribal healing practices, and the benefits of government welfare schemes specific to the Bedagampana Tribe. It will also focus on the Bedagampana's deep connection to the hills and its impact on their lifestyle and culture, the challenges faced by the Bedagampana in contemporary society, and the need for their assertion for inclusion in the Scheduled Tribes list and its potential implications.

Eight villages of Male Mahadeshwara hills have been taken as the locale of the study. Among the villages, Kaduhola has the highest frequency, representing 22.9 percent of the total households. This indicates that nearly a quarter of all instances fall into this category, making it the most prominent village. Following Kaduhola, Konganuru has a significant ratio of 19.0 percent of the total, thus showing it is also a major village taken as a sample. Tholasikare and Tammadagere also represent notable households i.e. 13.3 percent and 11.4 percent samples respectively. These four categories together account for a substantial majority of the data, at 66.6 percent. The remaining four categories—Marihola and Indiganatha each of 9.5 percent, Gorasane with 7.6 percent, and Keeranahola with 6.7 percent —comprise a smaller portion of the data. Collectively, they represent 33.4 percent of the total households. This distribution indicates a skewed concentration towards a few categories, particularly Kaduhola and Konganuru, suggesting that these villages had much more reachability in comparison to the others.

Similarly, the data represents the distribution of respondents across various age groups ranging from 25 to 80 years old. The age group with the highest frequency is 31–35 years, comprising 15.2 percent of the total. This is followed closely by the 56–60 age group, with respondents making up 14.3 percent. Other significant age groups included 36–40 and 46–50, each with 13.3 percent, and 41–45 with 12.4 percent. Interestingly, the younger age group of 25–30 years has the lowest frequency among the younger cohorts, with only 4.8 percent of the respondents. In contrast, the older age groups show a noticeable decline: the 61–65 age group included 7.6 percent (8 respondents), the 66–70 group with 8.5 percent of respondents, and both the 71–75 and 75–80 groups represented 1 percent of the 8 respondents. Overall, the age distribution highlights the predominance of middle-aged respondents among the surveyed sample.

Thus, the study gives a complete insight into the socio-cultural and economic aspects of the livelihood of the Bedagampana tribal community. The structure of this book on the Bedagampana tribe deals with an introduction, and etymology of the tribe, providing an overview of their geographic distribution, demographic details, and the significance of studying the Bedagampanas. It delves into the historical background, exploring their origins, early history, and evolution over time, including interactions with neighbouring communities. The socio-cultural aspects of the tribe are then examined, detailing their social structure, traditions, customs, rituals, festivals, and celebrations. Following this, the study focuses on their dietary practices, highlighting their predominantly vegetarian diet and its cultural and religious significance, while comparing it with the dietary practices of other tribes. The book is also dedicated to the Bedagampanas' convergence with the Veerashaiva and Lingayat communities, providing historical context for the merger, the socio-cultural practices leading to this integration, and its impact on their identity and traditions.

The connection to the hills, their geographic and environmental setting, the influence of the hills on their lifestyle and culture, and the spiritual and cultural significance of the natural environment have been studied in the book in detail to understand their specific cultural elements. Contemporary issues and challenges faced by the Bedagampanas are also assessed, focusing on their socio-economic challenges, access to education, healthcare, and economic opportunities, and efforts towards social and economic development. Finally, the book concludes with Bedagampana's assertion for inclusion in the Scheduled Tribes list, discussing the criteria for this status in India, the Bedagampanas' case for inclusion, and the potential benefits and implications of such recognition, providing a huge scope for researchers dealing with studies related to Indigenous people and complications related to tribal issues.

CHAPTER 2

Origin, History, and Oralities

Introduction

This chapter describes the history, evolution, and narratives of affection between the Bedagampana Community and Male Mahadeshwara Swamy. Male Mahadeshwara Swamy, revered as the 'God of poor people', is a spiritual figure who commands the devotion of millions. Despite this widespread reverence, the intricate relationship between Swamy Male Mahadeshwara and the Bedagampana community remains a lesser known yet profoundly significant narrative.

Historically, the Bedagampana tribal community has been the custodian of the traditions and rituals associated with Male Mahadeshwara Swamy. This unique bond is not merely a matter of religious duty but a deep-rooted cultural and spiritual connection that has evolved over centuries. The community's role in the temple rituals and their unwavering devotion to Swamy Male Mahadeshwara is pivotal in maintaining the sanctity and continuity of the traditions at Male Mahadeshwara Hills.

Male Mahadeshwara Swamy is considered an incarnation of Lord Shiva, known for his ascetic life and benevolence towards the poor and needy. The legend of Swamy Male Mahadeshwara is filled with tales of his miracles and his unwavering commitment to uplifting the marginalized. This narrative has been passed down through generations, creating a deep-rooted cultural ethos among his followers.

The Bedagampana tribal community, known for its dedication and service, has been bestowed with the unique privilege of conducting the primary rituals and poojas at the Male Mahadeshwara temple. This privilege is not just a religious duty but an honour that reflects their close association with the deity. The community's role in the temple is integral, as they are considered the direct link between Swamy Male Mahadeshwara and his devotees.

CHAPTER 2

Over the generations, as the gap between the old and the new widens, it becomes increasingly challenging to keep the traditions and culture of our roots intact. In this context, oral stories and historical narratives play a crucial role in bridging this gap. The tales of Male Mahadeshwara Swamy and the Bedagampana community's unwavering devotion serve as a reminder of the rich cultural heritage that needs to be preserved. The Male Mahadeshwara temple is not just a place of worship but a symbol of the enduring bond between the deity and his devotees. Every year, thousands of pilgrims from various parts of the country flock to the temple, seeking blessings and paying homage to Swamy Male Mahadeshwara. The rituals performed by the Bedagampana community are a testament to their deep-rooted faith and their commitment to preserving the age-old traditions.

Despite the large number of devotees who offer pooja to Swamy Male Mahadeshwara, very few attempts have been made to delve into the story behind the Bedagampana community's special role. This community's exclusive privilege to offer poojas and other rituals at the main temple is a significant aspect of their cultural identity. Understanding this relationship provides a deeper insight into the community's history, their evolution, and the affectionate narratives that bind them to Swamy Male Mahadeshwara. Hence, the chapter emphasizes the importance of preserving the cultural and spiritual heritage of the Bedagampana community and their unique bond with Male Mahadeshwara Swamy. Through oral stories and historical narratives, we can bridge the generational gap and ensure that the traditions and culture of our roots continue to thrive.

Origin and History

Bedagampana people are influenced by Veerashaiva principles and thereby adopted vegetarianism. Among Veerashaiva, there is a sect called Jangama. They are the spiritual guru and guide for Lingayat community. These Jangama gurus pay periodical visits to the houses of Lingayats in marriage ceremonies, naming ceremonies, housewarming ceremonies etc. The Lingayats washed their feet and used to drink the water, water with which they wash the feet of their gurus and according to them, it is considered as the teertha, which means holy water or the sacred water for drinking. These Veerashaiva Jangamas sought the help of Bedakampanaru, Kampana Bedaru or Bedagampana, to promote Veerashaivism i.e. the principles of Veerashaivas. To promote the principles of Veerashaivas, this Kampana Bedaru people want to describe themselves, and want to be called themselves, as the priest of Shiva. People used to say Beda is the term, derived from, the Sanskrit word, *vyadha* which means hunter. But Beda is a Dravidian word itself and an independent term. It is not derived from any other Sanskrit or any other language as such. In Dravidian, the word Beda means to pierce or trap (K.S. Singh, People of India, National Series, Volume II, page number 1367, Revised Edition, Anthropological Survey of India, 2010). Besides, Kampana means group or flock, or a sect, or clan, which means a group of hunters. Hence, Beda and Kampana are the two separate terms joined into one as Bedakampana. The contraction form of Beda and Kampana gives the term Bedakampana or Bedagampana in Kannada language. Kampana also connotes Kampala in Kannada which also means a *flock* of sheep, goats, cattle, and people.

There is another nomadic tribe, Bedajangamaru, or Budgajangamaru, which is a non-vegetarian community. Bedajangamas are religious mendicants and beggars. But the Bedajangama or Budga Jangama have not forbidden non-vegetarian dietary system. Whereas, the Bedagampana have forbidden their non-vegetarian dietary system. Bedagampanas are greatly influenced by Veerashaiva and Lingayat movements. The Veerashaiva movement was led by Renukacharya. Renukacharya was one among the *panchacharyas* (five Gurus). The Lingayat movement was led by Basavanna, the 770 Amarganas (the immortal saints), and 1,96,000 Vachanakaras (the saint poets). We do not see Vachanakaras in Veerashaiva. Bedagampanas are deeply influenced by the vegetarian principle of Veerashaivas. The people who come under the Lingayat movement are called Vachanakaras. According to some Vachanas of the Lingayat movement show that Lingayats did not forbid non-vegetarian dietary systems, but Veerashaivas have forbidden non-vegetarian. The examples can be found in the famous *Kalavve Vachana*. In one of the folksongs which has been frequently recited by the folksingers of Male Mahadeshwara tradition, we see the reflections of the characteristic features of Veerashaivas depicting Male Mahadeshwara.

Yelagavi Yeludoddu, Sulugaavi Musukittu
Korala Thumba Rudrakshi.
Mudina Paadakke Munnooru Jangu
Hindala Paadakke Innooru Jangu
Maikaigella Ibhuthi Dharsisikondu
Muthina Jolige Mungaige Aadhara Madkondu
Belli Betthavanna Balagaili Hidkondu
Honnuthadinda Hora Bandu Nintha Kallanne Baraga Madkondu

The above Kannada folksong tells us that, the folksingers have a perception of Male Mahadeshwara as Veerashaiva Jangama, decorated with anklet bells, holding silver cane, covering his head with the cloth, and armed with a begging

CHAPTER 2

bag, having a tiger as his escort. This picturization of Male Mahadeshwara by the folksingers carries the description as Jangama.

The notable fact here is that Bedagampana used to worship Male Mahadeshwara by offering meat as Naivaidya (the prasadam). These Bedagampana were earlier used to go for hunting and would kill wild bucks, wild sheep, rabbits, etc. They used to skin it, cut the meat, clean it, make dishes out of it, and offer the meat to Male Mahadeshwara as *Naivadya*. Later, with the influence of Veerashaiva Guru Panditaradhya (one of the *panchacharyas*), they forbade the practice.

In real terms, the 'Jangama' are the priests of the Shaiva community who provide services to Lingayats. Jangama is a religious sect. Bedagampana don't act as priests for Veerashaiva or Lingayats. But they go from village to village, taking the sacred bull with them. In Karnataka, the sacred bull is called 'Nandi Basava'. The people worship the bull believing it as the incarnation of Male Mahadeshwara and 'Tammadi', who acts as a priest and offers Pooja to Shiva, being a part of Bedagampana, they are religious and spiritual agents of Male Mahadeshwara. On the other hand, Veerashaiva Jangams among the Veerashaiva community go on preaching the principles of Veerashaivism assigned by their Pattadhikaris or the *panchacharyas* or the monastic centres. While Bedagampana do not go to the Lingayat houses as well as to the Veerashaiva houses, they were usually going to other communities and this duty was assigned to these Tammadis by the Veerashaivas. These Veerashaivas were the gurus at the monastic centres, and it highlights the major difference between the Veerashaiva Jangams and the Bedagampana. The Bedagampana went to other communities and propagated the principles of Veerashaiva Dharma. Even if they did not go, these Veerashaivas and Lingayats used to give alms to them to propagate their principles among other communities.

As stated earlier there was another nomadic tribe, Bedajangam or the Budgajangam. They are a nomadic tribe and also do begging. They are beggars by profession. But, now because of the laws enforced by the court and the government forbidding hunting to preserve forests and wild animals, these Bedajangam or the Budgajangam have given up hunting. But in the case of Bedagampana, they left hunting not because of the enforcement of the law by the government but it is because of the influence of the principles of Veerashaivism. That is how the Bedagampana is different from the Bedajangam or the Budgajangam. The Budga is a musical instrument. When they go for begging as they are street beggars, they used to play on Budga, a musical instrument. Especially the women, are the singers, folk singers, they used to play musical instruments like Tamburi, Gaggara, Dikki, Chitke, and Budhga and they used to sing Burra Kathalu, Budga Kathalu and so on. Even very recently, the Bedajangam community has been given the status of Scheduled Caste in Karnataka.

Being a nomadic tribe, Beda/Budga Jangama, we find that Jangama priests pay visits to the houses of the Madigas to offer their services at the death and marriage ceremonies. These Beda/Budga Jangamas are neither Veerashaiva nor Lingayats. Bedagampanas are migrated tribes from Srishailam, Srikakulam and Kalahasthi of Andhra Pradesh. Bedagampanas are different from the Veerashaiva community by their origin and practices. It is notable that, these Bedagampanas are the followers of Veerashaivisim. A Veerashaiva must strictly adhere to Ashtavarana or 8-fold protections. These Ashtavaranas are the religious rites of the Veerashaivas. The Ashtavaranas include 1. *Guru* (the teacher), 2. *Linga* (the symbol of Shiva) 3. *Vibhuti* (the sacred ash) 4. *Rudraksha* (the holy beads) 5. *Mantra* (chant) 6. *Jangam* (the moving Guru) 7. *Padodaka* (the water with which devotees wash the feet of their Guru) and 8. *Prasadam* (Holy food offered to God). The Veerashaiva Jangams after the birth of a child in a Lingayat family go to tie *linga* to that child. The ceremonious rite is called as *lingadharana*. The family headman of Lingayat family would send for the Jangama who might be a traditional religious advisor. The Veerashaiva Jangams are the spiritual masters frequently invited by the Lingayats whenever the Lingayats observe their religious rites in their houses and also at the time of the various ceremonies. The Veerashaiva Jangams go to the houses of Lingayats. But Lingayats do not go to the houses of Veerashaiva to offer these religious rites or services as Veerashaivas act as the highest in the social hierarchy. Lingayats do not go to Veerashaivas because Veerashaivas are Gurus and Lingayats are the followers. However, all those who joined the tradition of Veerashaivas, day by day, quite gradually, Lingayats and Veerashaivas are assimilated. Especially in the mutt culture. For example, Salur Mutt is the representative of *panchacharyas*. *Panchacharyas* do not consider Basavanna as their Guru.

In Kannada, *panchacharya* is a sectarian community having five Gurus or Acharyas. This community is spread in five places: Rambapuri, Ujjain, Kedar, Srishailam and Kashi. They are five Panchacharya Peethas meaning five monastic centres. In these five monastic centres, they have five Gurus: Revana Siddha (Renukacharya), Murula Siddha (Murularia), Ekorama Pandita, Panditaradhya, and Vishvaradhya. It is said that Revana Siddha is from Kuruba community (shepherds). Murula Siddha is from Madiga community (the leather workers). These *panchacharyas* are also known as Aaradhya Jangams.

Besides, the Jagamma who belong to Veerashaiva strictly adheres to Ashtavarana. They chant Panchakshari and Shatakshari Mantra. The Shatakshari and Panchakshari Mantra are *'Namah Shivaya'*, *'Om Namah Shivaya'* or *'Shivaya Namaha'*. Veerashaivas Jangams sarcastically claim themselves as 'Lingi Brahmins' whereas the Bedagampana claim themselves Scheduled Tribe. Apart from this, the fact that they don't have any kind of a mutual matrimonial relations, or they do not dine together also denotes them as separate community. The Bedagampana having adopted the principles of vegetarianism and wearing *linga* and sacred ash on their forehead adopted the principles of Veerashaivas. The Bedagampana takes the sacred bull while they go to get alms. The people believe that the sacred bull is the incarnation of Basavanna. As Basavanna was in 12th century and this Male Mahadeshwara was in 14th century, some of them also believe Male Mahadeshwara was an incarnation of Basavanna. They gave Basavanna the form of a bull and the horns of the bull are tied with the *linga* and metallic idol of Male Mahadeshwara.

Hence, the idol which is tied to the horns of the sacred bull symbolizes of Basavanna, the heroic figure of the 12th century and the *linga* symbolizes Male Mahadeshwara. And this Tammadi (a clan of Bedagampana) who used to carry the bull from house to house to receive alms are the agent of Male Mahadeshwara or the agent of Basavanna. The bull which they take out is decorated with many coloured clothes and Garland of notes are tied around the neck and to the horns of the bull. And people will come and stick the notes to that garland. The idol which is tied to the horns of the sacred bull symbolizes the cap, the sacred cap, which is put on by Basavanna.

Similarly, there is an another hunting community that later shifted to pastoral livelihood due to law enforcement, i.e. Myasa Beda community. Though they stopped hunting, they did not forbid eating non-vegetarian. In that community also, there are *Kilaris* (a clan – who do the duty of taking care of Sacred Bulls) as seen in Tammadis among Bedagampana. The kilaris of Myasa Beda also used to take the sacred bull to house to house, from street to street. The people believe that the sacred bull of the kilaris, resembles the Gadri Palanayaka, Kori Yeremanchanayaka, the tribal heroes of Myasa Beda Community. Whenever the bull is carried by kilaris, the sacred priests in the Myasa Beda community take this bull to the street, and the followers feel that Gadri Palanayaka, Yeremanchanayaka who were their ancestor hero has come out to the street. These sacred bulls are called Muthaiah. And the place where 'Muthaiah' (sacred bulls) sleeps, people will not enter with shoes as it is considered as a sacred place. The same can be seen in the Kadugolla community, forest gollas (who are known as Yadavas in many parts of India), the pujaris or the priests of the Kadugolla community take the sacred bulls to the streets for begging. And when Kadugolla priests, take the sacred bulls to the streets, the people feel that these bulls are ancestral heroes like Yettappa, Junjappa. Hence, these three communities are unique in taking the sacred bull for begging.

There are five major cattle herding or pastoral communities in Karnataka. They are: 1. Hallikar 2. Kadugolla 3. Kuruba 4. Kunchitiga and 5. Myasa Beda. But, if we look at Bedagampana, they are not a fully pastoral community, though they have a combined history with the Myasa Bedas. The Myasa Bedas are believed to be of Srishailam, Srikalahasti, and Srikakulam origin in Andhra Pradesh. Since they are a pastoral community, in search of food and water for their cattle, they came up to the hills of Male Mahadeshwara and Erode and Salem district of Tamil Nadu. It is also said that they have taken their journey to Nunkemale Siddheshwara hills (Central part of Karnataka) whereas one of their groups travelled via the Northern part of Karnataka to the banks of the Tungabhadra River. Interestingly Myasa Beda worshiped a deity named 'Kampanaranga' also known as 'Bedagampanaraya' or 'Veeragampanaraya'. It indicates all these downtrodden tribal communities share the same cultural ties. They have a great influence of the Veerashaiva community which can be denoted by the fact that while worshipping, the Myasa Bedaru people also do 'Bayikattu Puja' or 'Muchchu Puja' which refers to covering their mouth with a piece of cloth. The same tradition can be found among Tammadi clan of Bedagampana people. They practice this ritual while offering a Pooja and chanting mantras of Male Mahadeshwara to protect the sanctity of Male Mahadeshwara from their saliva.

However, it is seen in the Lingayat community that they believe saliva as a sacred element as it can be interpreted by taking the examples of one of the Vachanas of Basavanna. For example, it is believed when they offer *Tambula* or betel nut and betel leaves to Lord and if he chews and the spit comes to you it will be a sacred thing. Another reason behind this is they believe, 'jenu' i.e. honey is the leftover of honeybees, water on which we survive comprises saliva of aquatic animals, the milk has the saliva of calf, hence how saliva can be impure! This is one of the notions that differentiates Veerashaivas from Lingayats, though with the passing times both the communities had a cultural assimilation thus, started calling themselves as Veerashaiva Lingayat. However, the Bedagampana had a great influence of Veerashaivas on their culture.

As mentioned earlier above, Bedagampana or Kampanabedaru, are two terms, consisting of two common words, Beda and Kampana. Kampana or Kampala means *Mande* (flock) in Kannada language. For example, Kuri Mande (flock of sheep), Meke Mande (flock of goat), Danagala Mande (flock of cattle) etc. So, we may conclude that Kampana Bedas or Bedagampanas are *Kannadigas*. Kannada is their mother tongue. Myasa Bedas' mother tongue is Telugu/ Kannada and Kadugalla's mother tongue is Kannada, in whichever state they are settled. For example, Kampana Bedas or some people of Bedagampana are settled in Tamil Nadu, but their mother tongue is Kannada.

Even the totems of Bedagampana like Sore palu, Vana Hunase palu, Jambu Nerale palu etc. are exactly like totems of Bedas or Valmikis and Myasa Bedas.

CHAPTER 2

The totems of these forest tribes are related to fish, animals, trees, leaves, fruits, etc. depicting these tribes are worshippers of Mother Nature. Various totems like Jambunerale palu (sect of wild berries), Vanahunase palu (Sect of Dry Tamarind), Sore Palu (Sect of Ash gourd), Kuri Palu (Sect of Sheep), Bale Kuta Palu (Sect of Banana), Meenupalu (Sect of fish), Mavina Palu (Sect of Mangoes), Emmelaru Palu (Sect of Buffalo), etc. are in large numbers in Bedagampana, Valmiki and Myasa Bedas.

Bedagampanas have their own mutt culture which is influenced by Veerashaivism. These Kampana Bedas (Bedagampana) are very important to promote and preach the principles of Veerashaivism. But the same Kampana Bedas are inferior when it comes to enjoying social equality. Veerashaivas never give away or take the daughters from Bedakampanas/ Bedagampana in the marriages. They do not have wedlock with Veerashaiva or Lingayat communities because Veerashaivas/ Lingayats are considered superior, they enjoy high social status, and they look or treat Kampana Bedas as inferior to them. Thus, Bedagampana who are excluded by Veerashaivas is seen as economically undeveloped, herding the cattle, engaged as agricultural labourers, coolies, and less educated.

According to Veerashaivas, a Jangama is a Charamurthy. Chara means a perpetual movement or continuous movement. And this Charamurthy or Chara *linga* is a spiritual priest, who moves constantly, performing the religious rites. So, the Jangamas in the Veerashaiva community is described as 'moving *linga*'. This also has influenced the Bedagampana Community to uphold the principles and practices of Veerashaiva.

Male Mahadeshwara Hills is one of the well-known pilgrims situated in Hanur Taluk of Chamarajanagar District, Southern part of Karnataka. Shiva is the main deity of this sacred place, and it is called one of the most powerful places. Male Mahadeshwara Hills stretched its wider range between the border of Karnataka and Tamil Nadu. The Hill range contains nearly 77 Hills of namely Bheemana Kolli, Belada Kuppe, Kunturu Mutt, Mandi Gudde, Bandalli, Hanur, Ramapura, Kaudalli, Vadake Halli, Konana Kere, Thalu Betta, Thapsare, Kambada Boli, Kokka Bare, Halambaadi, Saluru Mutt, Nadugudi Basappa, Gaali Basappa, Katte Basaveshwara, Ishtarthasidhi Shile, Huri Kamba, Mahaganapathi, Sheshannodeyara Devalaya, Veereshwara Devalaya, Bomma Devaru, Karayya Billayana Kola, Jadekallu, Maharaja Chatra, Chandi Basappa, Oorakki Basava, Dundammana Gaddige, Ranagaswami Male, Shanka Male, Gunju Male, Paadadare, Kombudikki, Karayyana Boli, Beerayyana Boli, Hindi Basaveshwara, Halaruve Halla, Bermeshwara Devalaya, Martali – Sulavadi, Kichhugatthi Maramma, Bevina Kalammana Bayalu, Kembaalu Siddeshwara Devalaya, Devalyyana Boli, Huligudu Mahadeshwara, Kadeboli Veereshwara,

Mailumale Malleshwara, Nagamale, Aadimadappana Betta, Kenchu Male, Haleyuru Mata.

As history goes, Male Mahadeshwara is the flag bearer of Sharana Samskruthi and can be seen in the 14–15th century. Being a follower of Basavanna – a well-known saint of Karnataka who practiced and promoted *Sharana Samskruthi* to bring social change in the society. This movement is considered as revolutionary in awakening the people against the practice of untouchability, in equality and other social evils. He stood for 'Satya' (Truth), 'Dharma' (Religion), Ahimse (Nonviolence) and 'Samanathe' (Equality) in the society.

Folk songs and stories suggest that Male Mahadeshwara Swamy hailed from Uttama Pura, and there is also a saying that he hailed from near Srishaila in Andhra Pradesh. His parents, Chandrashekhara Murthy and Uttarajamma were blessed with his birth after many years through the blessings of Srishaila Mallikarjuna. Under the guidance of Sri Gnanananda Swamiji, Male Mahadeshwara traveled extensively to aid the sick, poor, and marginalized. His miracles during these travels left a lasting impact, and those places are still worshipped with great reverence.

Though he was named 'Marideva', later the name took the shape of Mahadeva (the Lord Shiva). There is this orality that says that Male Mahadeswara Swamy was moving on a tiger and performed many miracles around the hills to save the people and saints living there. The lord's miracles are beautifully sung by the village folk in 'Janapada' (folklore) style. According to legends, Male Mahadeswara was born in the 'Kaliyuga' to a fair-coloured virgin woman Uttarajamma. The then guru of Chandrashekara Murthy and Uttarajamma, Sri Gnanananda Swamiji influenced Swamy Male Mahadeshwara, under his direction and guidance he started to travel for the well-being of the people who were sick, poor, and unaccepted in the society. It is highly remarkable that wherever Male Mahadeshwara travelled he made his presence by doing many miracles. Even today those places are worshiped and guarded with utmost respect and devotion. In the meanwhile, Male Mahadeshwara Swamy wanted to get settled at a place he chose Male Mahadeshwara Hills for the rest of his life. This place is also called 'Dark State' or *kattaleya rajya*. To touch upon the Veerashaiva Movement which began under the leadership of Basavanna was also one of the reasons for Swamy Male Mahadeshwara to fight against the certain practices that were aiming to suppress the people. Contemporary to this time various other famous saints like Allamaprabhu, Basavanna, Akkamahadhevi, Channabhasavanna, and Siddharameshwara also sparked a sense of life among the deprived sections of the society. This gave rise to folk icons like Mahadeshwara (Madiga community), Manteswamy (Holeya community), 'Siddappaji', 'Junjappa' (cattle herder), and 'Mylara' (a shepherd).

CHAPTER 2

The epic of Male Mahadeshwara describes the life and miracles of the Saint. It is divided into seven parts and is sung by pilgrims on their way to the annual fair on the Male Madheshwara Hills. They are namely Thalugathe, Shravana Dore Salu, Junjegowdana Salu, Sankavvana Salu, Ikkeridevammana Salu, Saragurayyana Salu, and a few more. The professional singers of this epic are called 'Devara Guddaru' (God's children) and 'Kamsaleyavaru' (those singers who keep time with 'Kamsale' — bronze cymbals).

The deity who sleeps on Anemale (Elephant Hill)
He who drapes Jenu Male (Hill of Honey Bees)
He who has intertwined all seventy-seven hills and condensed them into a pillow
Let's all hail our beloved father "Moodalu Madeva's"
Let's all hail our beloved father's feet. (Rajashekar, 1973, p.26)

"Maleya Madeshwara"

Eventually, Male Mahadeshwara Swamy chose the Male Mahadeshwara Hills, once known as the 'dark state' and also as Vajra Male, as his permanent residence. The deep-rooted connection between the Bedagampana community and Soligas is often described in various oral stories like the story of Karayya-Billayya, Neelayya, etc.

According to these oral stories, in the serene forest area of Male Mahadeshwara Hills, Soligara Neelayya and his wife, the beautiful Sankamma, lived a life intertwined with nature. One day, Neelayya set out for hunting, leaving Sankamma behind. Before he left, he became consumed by suspicion regarding Sankamma's chastity and forced her to swear fidelity. This led to a heated argument between them. In a fit of rage and mistrust, Neelayya resorted to cruel methods, using black magic mantras and tantras to imprison Sankamma. Heartbroken and in pain, Sankamma began to weep and chant the name of Male Mahadeshwara.

Her cries reached the divine ears of Swamy Male Mahadeshwara, who then appeared before her. After hearing her tragic tale, Swamy Male Mahadeshwara decided to free her from torment. In his compassion, Swamy Male Mahadeshwara blessed Sankamma with two sons, Karayya and Billayya. As the boys grew, their paths diverged by the divine will. Karayya, who did not heed the words of Male Mahadeshwara, strayed from the given guidance and became known as Soligas. He and his descendants adopted a lifestyle that included eating non-vegetarian food, a practice they have followed ever since. On the other hand, Billayya, who faithfully followed Male Mahadeshwara's teachings, became a devoted disciple. He renounced non-vegetarian food and led a life of piety, eventually giving rise to the Bedagampana community. According to another oral story of Karayya-Billayya, it has been flowing through generations. Here is a small experience of Male Mahadeshwara with Bedara Kannappa. Male Mahadeshwara after encountering the renowned hunter Bedara Kannappa, Mahadeva makes him his disciple by demonstrating his hunting abilities in a duel. Upon learning about a villain named Shravana Dhore (king), Mahadeva, along with his new team, devises a plan to put an end to his tyranny. They skilfully trap the Shravana king and burn down his palace, thereby freeing the 300 gods he had imprisoned. There is a mention of these names Karayya and Billayya in the book *Caste and Tribes of Southern India*, Volume -VII – T – Z, 1909 by Thurston E. and Rangachari K.

The Bedagampana Community is a small tribal group residing at the foothills of Male Mahadeshwara Hills in Hanur Taluk, with some members also living in parts of Tamil Nadu. With a history spanning 600 years, their existence is documented in inscriptions such as Haradanalli inscription, Haidarali inscription, and Veera Ballala inscription. Traditionally, hunters, the Bedas live in forests and engage in forest-based activities for their livelihood. Hardanahalli was the secondary capital of a Hoysala feudatory ruling the region called Ennenadu. Early records of Ballala III dated A.D. 1340 refer to the place as Mageya. A spurious copper plate record (dated 1345) of the same period mentions the place as Vanijyaouri. In Mysore Chapter 1988 report writes about the Divya Lingeshwara temple that was originally built by Ballala III in A.D. 1316 and later improved by Vijayanagara and Mysore rulers. The pillars of the frontal *manatapa* contain fine relief sculptures like those of Bedara Kannappa, Bhakta Markandeyam Siriyala, Shiva Tandava etc. This stands as evidence of the existence of Bedara Kannappa and his achievements in those times and few inscriptions like this give some sort of clarity that Bedagampana is a tribe.

Influence of Swamy Male Mahadeshwara

Swamy Male Mahadeshwara profoundly influenced the Bedagampana Community. According to oral traditions, when Swamy Male Mahadeshwara arrived at Male Mahadeshwara Hills, he encountered the Soligas and Bedagampana communities living in isolation away from civilized society. Swamy Male Mahadeshwara aimed to reform these communities by teaching them rituals and practices akin to Sharana Samskruthi or Veerashaiva culture. Such examples are found in the book of David Hardiman 'The Coming of the Devi: Adivasi Assertion in Western India' (1987). The book describes a similar kind of movement called 'Devi' in Western India where the *Devi/Goddess* called 'Salabai' was centred as a point of socio-cultural transformation of tribal people residing in Palghar of Southern Gujarat of India in1920s. The movement was basically to get rid of the Sahukars

CHAPTER 2

(rich people) and the Parsi community (liquor manufactures) but later it mobilized them with new cultural ethos that included 'no alcohol, vegetarianism, non-violence, cleanliness, boycott of the Parsis' (Chaudhari, 2018). The Bedagampana tribe also went through a similar reformation where the primarily hunting tribe was highly influenced by the words of the Swamy Male Mahadeshwara, according to the community leaders of the Bedagampana.

In recognition of their devotion and the changes they embraced, Swamy Male Mahadeshwara decreed that only members of the Bedagampana Community would be privileged to offer pooja to him after his deification. This exclusive privilege continues to strengthen the bond between the Bedagampana tribal community and Swamy Male Mahadeshwara, preserving their traditions and cultural heritage.

Swamy Male Mahadeshwara's mission to integrate the Bedagampana Community into the Veerashaiva Culture was significantly supported by Salur Mutt (Kuntur Mutt). Salur Mutt, considered the backbone of the community, continues to play a crucial role in upholding the community's rituals, practices, and decisions.

The Role of Salur Mutt

Salur Mutt has played a crucial role in preserving the cultural and spiritual heritage of the Bedagampana people. The establishment of the Mutt by Lord Mahadeshwara himself and making the Bedagampana families as the hereditary 'Archaks' (Priests) gave them the rights to perform daily rituals, special poojas, and ceremonies during festivals, maintaining an unbroken lineage of service to Male Mahadeshwara Swamy. The Mahadeshwara temple, which is the main worshipping institution for the Bedagampana, was under the control and management of Sri Salur Mutt, until it was handed over to the Madras Government in 1953. This transition marked a significant shift in the administrative and operational aspects of the temple but did not diminish the influence of Salur Mutt on the Bedagampana community.

Even today, all significant rituals, practices, and decisions concerning the Bedagampana Community are conducted under the auspices of Salur Mutt. This institution remains central to the community's spiritual and social life, ensuring the continuity of the traditions introduced by Swamy Male Mahadeshwara. As the spiritual headquarters, the Mutt oversees the religious activities and ensures that the traditional practices are meticulously followed. The Mutt has been instrumental in educating the community about their heritage, reinforcing the teachings of Veerashaivism and miracles of Swamy Male Mahadeshwara.

Structure of the Bedagampana Community

The Bedagampana Community is structured into nearly 48 clans, which are sub-groups within the community. A notable aspect of their cultural practice is the mandatory wearing of the *linga* – a Shivalinga idol worn in a holy thread. This practice signifies their adherence to the Veerashaiva tradition and their devotion to Lord Shiva, as guided by Swamy Male Mahadeshwara. The major among them are Dodda Palu (Big Flock), Chikka Palu (Small Flock), and Kaduveerana Palu (Group of Forest Heroes). Doddapalu has families namely Pakshi Manethana (Lineage of Birds), Kudduvayya Manethana, Kotturan Manethana, and two more. Whereas Chikkapalu has families like Marigudi Manethana, Tamboori (musical instrument) Manethana, Masinakeri Manethana, Gowdana Keri Manethana, Chelubasappa Manethana. Lastly, Kaduveeranapalu has only one family.

Every family of three Clan will take turns performing poojas at the Male Mahadeshwara temple once every 4 months, and one person will receive an honorarium for their duties. The Male Mahadeshwara Development Authority covers these expenses. Vibrant cultural traditions associated with the worship of Male Mahadeshwara Swami at the Male Mahadeshwara Hills. These festivals and rituals, such as Halaravi Seve (Service of Pot of Milk), Puduvina Pooje, Deepavali (Festival of Lights), Ugadi (New Year of Hindus), and Yenne Majjana (Oil Bath), hold significant spiritual importance for the devotees. Once a year, they have the ritual of Climbing Hills i.e. Pandeshwara and Baraguru Betta (Hills), they all dress up as Beda's and they do some festivities. They distribute food to all the people in the name of Male Mahadeshwara.

The Tammadi clan, known for their strict adherence to ritual practices, has been preserving these traditions for centuries. Each of these festivals and rituals has its unique customs and significance. The Male Mahadeshwara Hills attracts many devotees who participate in these events with devotion and enthusiasm, maintaining a deep connection to their cultural and religious heritage.

Summary

The Bedagampana Community is originally from a forest-culture background. Their history speaks volumes of their existence in society. Male Mahadeshwara's oral stories as they flourish through folk songs, folk stories, dramas, and other various forms of art, these Bedagampanas have become the soul of it. Male Mahadeshwara miracles and feats of magic have made people attracted. At a young age, he started a pathway of spirituality and made sure that he upheld the *truth, dharma, and equality*. He travelled to many places by preaching and promoting good things and made his legacy to be prayed by everyone in their way. Each story of his still makes people to the deepest devotion. Male Mahadeshwara and Bedagampana are blended in a soulful way. He gained many followers through his divine acts and those who witnessed him would turn into his disciples, this is how Mahadeshwara is described. The Bedagampana community never claimed that they are Lingayat's, yet they are called Bedagampana Lingayat for various reasons. Bedagampana community is the only community that is privileged in offering poojas to Male Mahadeshwara in a unique way. This indicates the bonding shared between the *Holy Man* Male Mahadeshwar and *the Hunters* of Bedagampana Community at Male Mahadeshwara Hills.

CHAPTER 3

Socio-Economic Conditions and Dietary Practices

Introduction

This chapter explains the Socio-Economic background of the Bedagampana community and also importantly their dietary practices. The chapter has several factors that reflect their present status in this advanced scenario. Healthy living is not only mere physical and mental health, but social health is also getting its priority. The socio-economic background indicates the present condition of the Bedagampana community and their quality of life. Traditionally, the Bedagampana community has relied heavily on agriculture as their primary means of subsistence. Their farming practices, deeply rooted in tradition, involve the use of age-old techniques and tools passed down through generations. These practices are typically sustainable and closely aligned with the natural environment, promoting biodiversity and ecological balance. The crops they cultivate include a variety of grains, vegetables, and legumes, which are integral to their diet and way of life. Meanwhile, their food habits are unique and differ from other tribes who are living in other parts of the country and also in the globe. Since they call themselves 'vegetarian', it shows the practices that are from the past. The dietary practices of the Bedagampana Community are a testament to their cultural heritage and ecological adaptation. This vegetarianism is not merely a dietary choice but a reflection of their deep-rooted cultural and spiritual beliefs. Historically, their diet has been heavily reliant on locally grown fruits, vegetables, grains, and legumes, which are cultivated using sustainable agricultural practices. Seasonal variations play a significant role in their diet, with different fruits and vegetables being consumed according to their availability. These are the witnesses that may help us to explore more in-depth study about

CHAPTER 3

the Bedagampana community. Further, whenever one talks about the custom, ritual and way of life of indigenous people, it becomes very important to know the perspective of the community people itself along with the reflections of the researcher. Hence, this chapter tries to discuss their life, livelihood, land holdings, their social and cultural beliefs. It is also an attempt to understand the lifestyle of Bedagampana from their perspective.

Family, Land and Living Conditions
Family

This gives a view of villages/hamlets where Bedagampana community people are living. The provided data summarizes the frequency and distribution of samples across eight distinct villages. Kaduhola has the highest frequency representing 22.9 percent of the total. This indicates that nearly a quarter of all instances fall into this category, making it the most prominent village. Following Kaduhola, Konganuru has a significant frequency making up 19.0 percent of the total, thus showing it is also a major village taken as sample. Tholasikere and Tammadigere also show notable frequencies 13.3 percent and 11.4 percent samples respectively. These four categories together account for a substantial majority of the data, at 66.6 percent. The remaining four categories—Marihola and Indiganatha each with 9.5 percent, Gorasane with 7.6 percent, and Kiranahola with 6.7 percent —comprise a smaller portion of the data. Collectively, they represent 33.4 percent of the total households. This distribution indicates a skewed concentration towards a few categories, particularly Kaduhola and Konganuru, suggesting that any interventions, resources, or analyses might benefit from focusing on these major groups.

This highlights the family names that are in the Bedagampana Community. The dataset presents the frequency distribution of two categories: 'Gowda' and 'Tammadi'. Out of this Gowda has a frequency accounting for 11.4 percent of the total instances. Tammadi has a significantly higher frequency representing 88.6 percent of the total making it the predominant category within the dataset. Tammadis are the only ones who privilege to offer pooja to Swamy Male Mahdeshwara at Male Mahadeshwara Hills. In Tammadis again they are categorized into three parts i.e. Dodda Palu, Chikka Palu, and Kaduveerana Palu.

Surprisingly, in the given dataset, women account for 22.9 percent of the total while Men are making up 77.1 percent of the total. This analysis highlights a predominant trend of men being the head of the family, comprising more than three-quarters of the sample, while less than a quarter of the heads of families are women. This gender-based distribution may reflect traditional family roles or other socio-cultural factors influencing the designation of the head of the family within the surveyed population. Women in Bedagampana are actively involved in playing significant roles in determining household affairs, family dynamics, and welfare.

When it comes to family structure, joint families account for representing 64.8 percent of the total, and nuclear families are represented by making up 35.2 percent of the total. The data reveals a clear dominance of joint families over nuclear families. The higher frequency of joint families could reflect cultural norms or traditions where extended family living arrangements are common.

This paragraph explains the size of the family where analysis shows that single-member households predominantly consist of adults, with males slightly outnumbering females. As the number of household members increases, the distribution of male and female adults remains relatively balanced, but the number of children fluctuates. Notably, there are fewer female children compared to male children in the overall sample. Larger households (five or more members) are rare, and unique family structures can be observed in six and seven-member households. This distribution reflects a variety of household compositions within the surveyed population.

Land

The data on land ownership reveals critical insights into the economic status and stability of the households surveyed. A substantial majority, 81.0 percent, have owned land, indicating a strong prevalence of land ownership within the community. This high percentage suggests that land ownership is a significant factor in the community's economic foundation, potentially providing these households with resources for agriculture, housing stability, and economic security. Conversely, 19.0 percent do not own land, representing a minority within the sample. This group may face more economic vulnerability and instability, lacking the security and potential income that land ownership can provide. This analysis indicates that while the majority of the community benefits from the economic advantages of land ownership, a notable minority still lacks this critical asset, which reflects broader issues of economic inequality and access to resources within the population.

Size of Land Holdings: The data on the size of the land owned by the surveyed population provides a detailed view of land distribution. A notable portion, 38.1 percent, own 2 acres of land, representing the largest group within the sample. This indicates a common landholding size that may support moderate agricultural activities or provide a stable foundation for economic sustenance. Following this, 26.7 percent own 1 acre of land. This smaller landholding size suggests a segment of the population with limited agricultural or economic potential, likely facing more constraints in land use and productivity. Additionally, 16.2 percent own between 3 to 5 acres, indicating a group with relatively larger landholdings, which could signify greater economic stability and the potential for more substantial agricultural output or investment opportunities. Conversely, 19.0 percent are categorized as 'Not Available', which corresponds to the previously identified group that does not own land. This reinforces the finding that a significant minority within the community lacks land ownership, highlighting issues of economic disparity. Overall, this analysis reveals Bedagampana with a significant variation in landholding sizes, predominantly owning small to moderate-sized plots, with a notable portion of the population still without land, reflecting ongoing economic inequalities.

Type of Land: The data on the type of land provides further insight into the nature of land owned by the surveyed population. The majority, 71.5 percent, own 'wet land', which is typically more fertile and suitable for agriculture, indicating that most landowners have potentially productive land capable of supporting various crops and contributing to better economic stability. In contrast, 9.5 percent own 'dry land', which is less fertile and may be more challenging to cultivate. This group likely faces more significant agricultural challenges and economic constraints due to the lower productivity of their land. This analysis indicates that while a substantial majority of the land-owning population has access to fertile, productive land, a smaller segment owns less productive dry land, and a significant minority remains without any land. This distribution reflects varying levels of agricultural potential and economic well-being within the community, with land quality playing a crucial role in determining individual economic stability.

Living Conditions

The data on the type of house provides insights into the living conditions of the sample population. A majority, 62.9 percent, reside in Kuccha or temporary houses, which are typically made from mud, thatch, or other locally available materials. This suggests a prevalence of semi-permanent housing structures within the community, likely indicative of lower socioeconomic status and limited access to durable housing materials. In contrast, 30.5 percent live in Pucca houses, which are constructed with more permanent materials like brick, cement, or concrete, reflecting a higher standard of living and better economic stability. A small percentage, 6.7 percent, reside in 'huts', the most rudimentary form of housing, often associated with the poorest segments of the population. This analysis suggests Bedagampana as a community predominantly living in less durable housing, with a significant portion having access to more stable, permanent housing, highlighting varying levels of economic well-being.

The data on the number of rooms in houses provides an additional layer of understanding about the living conditions of the respective households in the sample. A significant portion, 42.9 percent, live in houses with two rooms, indicating a common housing size that likely accommodates the basic needs of an average family. Following this, 21.0 percent live in three-room houses, suggesting a segment of the population with relatively more space and potentially better living conditions. Meanwhile, 20.0 percent reside in one-room houses, reflecting a notable fraction of the population experiencing more constrained living conditions, which may be indicative of larger families sharing minimal space or households with limited economic means. A smaller group, 16.1 percent, lives in four-room houses, representing the more affluent segment within the community, capable of affording more spacious living arrangements. This analysis reveals a community with a diverse range of housing sizes, where the majority live in moderately sized homes, but a significant number still face limited living space, underscoring the variability in economic conditions and housing adequacy.

Further, the Bedagampana possess various livestock for their dietary and religious purposes. The livestock are valued for their milk, which can be a crucial source of nutrition. Milk and milk products can form a substantial part of the tribe's diet, and cows also hold cultural or religious significance, often revered and protected in many vegetarian and agrarian societies. They are also likely used for plowing and other heavy farm work, essential in a community that relies on agriculture. The large number of households involved in livestock ownership suggests more affluent or agriculturally active members of the tribe. In summary, within a vegetarian tribe like Bedagampana, the ownership patterns of domestic animals support their agricultural lifestyle, highlighting the multifaceted roles that these animals play in nutrition, farming, and economic stability.

Though some of the Bedagampana houses are currently managing some form of financial obligation in terms of debts or loans, a larger segment has managed to avoid taking on such liabilities. Among those who did report taking out loans, agriculture emerged as the primary reason. Others include loans for healthcare, business ventures, or personal expenses which are almost negligible. This highlights the importance of credit in supporting agricultural activities, which are often capital-intensive and subject to various economic and environmental risks.

CHAPTER 3

Occupations

This explains a detailed frequency distribution of respondents' occupations, offering insights into the diverse range of professions represented in the data:

- Coolie: This category accounts for the largest proportion of respondents at 39.0 percent.
- Labour: Following closely, labourers constitute 23.8 percent of the respondents, highlighting a significant presence of manual labour roles.
- Driver: 7.6 percent identified as drivers, indicating a notable representation in transportation-related occupations.
- Agriculture: 6.7 percent work in agriculture, reflecting the prevalence of farming as a livelihood.
- Farmer and Temple worker: Each category represents 5.7 percent, showcasing the diversity of traditional and religious occupations.

Other professions such as business owners, security guards, and government employees are represented but in smaller numbers. Notably, there is a single response for some categories like chef, hospital worker, and watchman. The data underscores occupational diversity encompassing both traditional sectors like agriculture and emerging roles in business and services. Labour-intensive roles like the prominence of roles like coolie and labourer highlight the prevalence of manual labour occupations among respondents.

Gender of Employees

Among the employees surveyed, 95.2 percent are male, while 4.8 percent are female. This data illustrates a significant gender disparity within the surveyed workforce, with a substantial majority of male employees compared to their female counterparts. This gender imbalance may reflect broader societal trends or specific industry dynamics influencing employment opportunities for men and women. This data highlights the need for organizations and policymakers to implement strategies that foster gender diversity and inclusivity in the workplace, ultimately leading to more equitable and inclusive employment practices.

Main Occupation

The majority of the respondents comprising 84.8 percent, stated that their main occupation is agriculture. This dominance of agricultural work within the surveyed population suggests a strong reliance on farming or related agricultural activities for livelihoods. Additionally, 15.2 percent reported being 'coolie' as their primary occupation. The smaller representation of 'coolie' suggests that such occupations are also present among the tribal group though less compared to agricultural work.

Among the respondents, the majority, accounting for 52.4 percent, indicated Male Mahadeshwara as their place of work. This suggests a significant concentration of employment opportunities or economic activity in the Male Mahadeshwara Hills area like the works related to the temple or other ancillary works within the surveyed population. Additionally, 23.8 percent reported working in Bangalore, indicating a notable presence of employment opportunities in the city. Furthermore, 14.3 percent mentioned Tamil Nadu as their place of work, followed by 6.7 percent in Mysuru and 2.9 percent in Andhra Pradesh. This data provides insights into the geographical distribution of employment among the surveyed population, highlighting key areas where households are engaged in work activities and the preferences of the locals for further migration. A significant factor here is that within the surveyed population, there are no households who acknowledge being unemployed, making the rate of unemployment zero percentage.

Migratory and Modern Economic Activities

Family members migrated indicates that 22.9 percent reported instances of migration within their families. This suggests a noteworthy degree of mobility within the surveyed population. Conversely, the majority, comprising 77.1 percent of respondents, stated that no family members had migrated. The presence of migration highlights a notable degree of mobility, potentially driven by factors such as economic opportunities and better living facilities. Conversely, the majority reporting no migration suggests a prevalence of rootedness or stability within the community, possibly due to strong ties to the local area, stable employment, or cultural preferences for remaining close to family and tradition.

The data shows that 77.1 percent reported that migration did not occur within the majority of surveyed households. However, 21 percent reported one instance of migration from a single family, while a smaller proportion of 1.9 percent reported two instances of migration. This distribution suggests that while the majority of families did not experience migration, there is a subset within the surveyed population where migration from a single family has occurred, with some households experiencing multiple instances of migration.

All instances of migration are related to the occupation of 'labourer', with 22.9 percent reporting this as the occupation associated with migration. This finding highlights the significant mobility among labourers, likely driven by the search for better employment opportunities, higher wages, or more stable work conditions. Labour migration is often a response to economic necessity, with households seeking work in areas with higher demand for labour, potentially leading to improved living standards for their families. This data underscores the importance of addressing these factors through targeted policies and programs, such as job creation, skills training, and improved labour market conditions, can help manage and support the mobility of labourers, ensuring they can find gainful employment without the need for frequent migration.

It is observed that there is a dominant non-migratory behaviour within the population, with a smaller, yet significant, fraction engaging in seasonal migration. It suggests Bedagampana as a predominantly stable community with a minor, but crucial, segment adapting to seasonal demands or opportunities, which reflects the socioeconomic dynamics and employment patterns influencing migration behaviour. The pattern of seasonal migration observed suggests that summer might be a peak period for returning to the houses due to factors such as the end of agricultural or construction seasons.

The data on migrating states shows that 77.1 percent reported 'Not Applicable', indicating no migration. Among those who did report migration, Tamil Nadu is the primary destination 20.9 percent moving there. Additionally, 1.0 percent migrated to Andhra Pradesh and Kerala. This indicates that Tamil Nadu is a significant destination for migrants within the surveyed population, likely due to better employment opportunities and its nearby geographical location. The smaller numbers migrating to Andhra Pradesh and Kerala suggest these states are fewer common destinations but still relevant for certain households. Understanding the migration patterns reveals that a substantial portion of the population seeks opportunities outside their home state, with Tamil Nadu being particularly attractive. This can be indicative of the geographical preference, socio-economic conditions, and opportunities in Tamil Nadu that draw migrants, possibly including higher wages, more job availability, and better living conditions compared to their home regions. The low numbers for Andhra Pradesh and Kerala indicate limited but specific reasons for migration to these states, which could be explored further to understand the unique opportunities they present.

Dietary Practices

The primary study on the dietary practices of the Bedagampana Community reveals that all family members in the surveyed population practice a vegetarian diet, indicating a uniform dietary preference within the households. This finding suggests a cultural or lifestyle choice towards vegetarianism, potentially influenced by factors such as religious beliefs, which is also beneficial in terms of health considerations, or environmental concerns making them the only existing vegetarian tribal group.

Practicing Vegetarian Diet – in years

It emphasizes prevalent and long-standing adherence to a vegetarian diet among the surveyed population. An overwhelming majority, comprising 93.3 percent, reported practicing vegetarianism for over 50 years, indicating a deeply ingrained dietary habit within the community. This long-term commitment to vegetarianism likely reflects cultural, religious, or ethical beliefs passed down through generations. Additionally, a small proportion reported practicing vegetarianism for 10–20 years (4.8 percent) and 20–30 years (1.9 percent), indicating a minority who adopted vegetarianism relatively recently. This data is mainly reported among the youth respondents. The data underscores the enduring popularity and cultural significance of vegetarian diets within the surveyed population, highlighting the potential influence of Veerashaiva and Lingayats among the Bedagampana tribal group.

Diets Related to Seasonal Change

Respondents are adhering to diets related to seasonal changes, indicating a widespread practice within the surveyed population. This suggests a cultural tradition of adjusting dietary habits based on the seasonal availability of food, likely influenced by factors such as agricultural practices, climate, and cultural customs. Such dietary adaptations may contribute to nutritional diversity and overall well-being by aligning food consumption with seasonal produce and local resources.

Special Food Practices Season Wise

This indicates that among the surveyed population, special food practices related to seasonal changes are prevalent. The majority, comprising 90.5 percent, reported consuming ragi laddoos, likely during specific seasons when ragi (a type of millet) is abundant and traditionally consumed. Additionally, smaller proportions reported consuming mango (2.8 percent) and jackfruit (6.7 percent), suggesting a cultural tradition of incorporating seasonal fruits into the diet. These practices reflect a connection between dietary habits and seasonal availability of food, highlighting the cultural significance of adapting food consumption patterns to environmental changes. Such practices not only contribute to nutritional diversity but also underscore the importance of sustainability and locality in food choices.

One of the unique aspects of their dietary practices is the use of wild foods. The Bedagampana community has a profound knowledge of edible plants and herbs found in their surrounding forests. These wild foods not only add nutritional value to their diet but also have medicinal properties, contributing to their overall health. Their vegetarianism is also influenced by their spiritual and cultural practices. Many rituals and festivals involve the preparation and consumption of specific vegetarian dishes, which are considered sacred. This aspect of their dietary practice reinforces their identity and fosters a sense of community.

Summary

Bedagampana Community is the most backward community in terms of their socio-economic status. The Bedagampana Community presents a fascinating case study in the intersection of socio-economic conditions, cultural practices, and dietary habits. Analysing their socio-economic background reveals a community deeply rooted in traditional agricultural practices, yet slowly transitioning to diversified occupational roles. Agriculture remains a significant aspect of their livelihood, but the allure of urban employment and modern economic opportunities is beginning to reshape their economic landscape. This shift is indicative of broader trends seen in rural and tribal India, where traditional ways of life are being augmented by the prospects of better wages and living conditions in urban settings. However, this transition also poses challenges, such as the potential loss of traditional knowledge and the erosion of cultural practices. Family structure and size are shown significant among Bedagampana as they have a joint family system to an extent and the headship is in the hands of the men. They are migratory in characteristics and seasonal in gaining their steady income. Agriculture is indeed the main occupation as they practice it as a traditional occupation, and they have very little land holding which may not yield better agricultural production. The present generation is moving towards jobs that may not fetch a good amount of income as they are not highly qualified in their education. It is highly notable that in spite of being in the woods for centuries, they are practicing vegetarianism. We have multiple examples that prove people who live in forests have a habit of consuming non-vegetarian food and mild consumption of vegetarian food. However, the Bedagampana community stands unique in this way. As this chapter gives an overview of the general lifestyle of the Bedagampana tribal people, it becomes important to understand how culturally they are different from the other tribal groups or the neighbouring communities like Veerashaiva and Lingayats. The following chapter is a discussion of the same which tries to explore the reasons behind the cultural transition, assimilation, and differentiation of the Bedagampana as a unique tribe. The chapter is a combination of both the observations made by the researchers and the results of the discussions derived from the community people and the leaders in the primary survey.

CHAPTER 4

Cultural Practices and Beliefs

Introduction

The Bedagampana, an indigenous tribe embodies a vibrant confluence of cultural, religious, and social traditions. Despite their distinct identity and rich heritage, the Bedagampana struggle for recognition and inclusion in the official Scheduled Tribes list, often being overshadowed by the larger Lingayat community. This chapter explores the unique aspects of Bedagampana culture, focusing on their cultural expressions, rituals, traditions, and the interplay of religion and spirituality that defines their way of life.

The Bedagampana maintain their cultural knowledge and identity through a strong oral tradition, with storytelling. It is part of their non-material culture and plays a crucial role in the preservation of history. Their folklore, music, and dance are integral to their cultural expressions, often involving community participation and deep spiritual significance. Non-material practices, such as various ceremonies and rites of passage, reinforce social bonds and spiritual connections within the community.

Rituals and traditions are central to Bedagampana, marking important life events and emphasizing cultural values. Practices surrounding pregnancy, childbirth, marriage, and death highlight the community's deep-rooted beliefs and the significance they place on these milestones. These traditions not only foster social cohesion but also preserve the cultural identity of the Bedagampana.

Similarly, religion and spirituality are foundational to the Bedagampana way of life, providing meaning and purpose to their rituals and traditions. Their spiritual practices reflect a worldview that emphasizes divine protection, moral righteousness, and the pursuit of salvation. Despite sharing some religious practices with the Veerashaivism and Lingayat community, the Bedagampana maintain distinct customs and beliefs that underscore their unique cultural identity.

The Bedagampana's identity crisis is further complicated by their historical and cultural connections with the Veerashaiva and Lingayats. While there are shared religious elements, significant differences in rituals and customs highlight their distinctiveness. The Bedagampana's inclusion in the Veerashaiva Lingayat category of the backward community list has led to their marginalization, depriving them of the benefits accorded to recognize Scheduled Tribes by the constitution.

Hence, this chapter will look into the Bedagampana community's rich cultural heritage and distinct identity that deserve unique recognition and support. Addressing their challenges requires an understanding of their cultural expressions, religious beliefs, and the socio-political dynamics that affect their existence.

Cultural Expressions

The cultural expressions of society are denoted by its art, music, dance, folklore, and non-material practices. Bedagampana as an Indigenous tribe is also characterized by unique cultural expressions. Their cultural elements are different forms of storytelling and preserving history. Folklores are a vital aspect of Bedagampana culture, passed down orally through generations. These stories often feature gods, spirits, and ancestral heroes, providing moral lessons and explanations of natural phenomena. The oral tradition ensures the continuity of their cultural knowledge and identity. Non-material practices, such as rituals and ceremonies, are integral to the Bedagampana way of life. These practices often involve offerings to deities, community feasts, and rites of passage, reinforcing social bonds and spiritual connections. Through their art, music, dance, folklore, and non-material practices, the Bedagampana maintains a vibrant and resilient cultural heritage.

The present form of Bedagampana folklore is sung in the Janapada folklore style. The existing form of Bedagampana folklore is mainly based on the legends of Male Mahadeshwara. Keshavan Prasad. *et. Al.* (2001) state:

> The singers of this epic are variously known as 'Guddaru' and 'Devara Guddaru' [Gods' Children], and 'Kamsaleyavaru' [those that sing to the rhythm of 'Kamasale' [bronze cymbals] and Dambadige (small tambourine).

They further describe,

> The vocabulary of this dialect, mostly, is different from standard Kannada, and the performers avoid partaking in any non-vegetarian food and liquor. The singers of the narrative number three to five, of whom one is the lead singer control and shape the course of the performance in a stylized tone. The other singers (their part in the performance is called 'Sollu') function as both 'audience' and chorus: during the narration of the prose part, at the end of each line they clang the cymbals, and add words of assent or reinforcement.

Similarly, they practice *Maari Kunitha* as their special dance form. It involves rhythmic movements accompanied by traditional music, performed during occasions and celebrations. This dance not only entertains but also displays their heritage, symbolizing unity and community spirit among the Bedagampana. Special fairs are observed in the months of Sravana (monsoons) which are the months of Lord Shiva and accordingly, they hail *Badavara Devaru Madappa* meaning 'Mahadeshwara, the lord of the poor people' which is the regional name of Lord Shiva in the Male Mahadeshwar Hills.

In the cultural expressions of Bedagampana women play an important role. In the folklore and oral epics sung in praise of Male Mahadeshwar Swamy, various women play a lead role. This includes the mention of women like Kalamma, and Sankamma, who embody strength, virtue, and resilience. This represents that in the cultural expressions of the Bedagampana, women hold a central and influential role, reflecting the dynamics of a matrilineal society. Their stories reflect the broader cultural values and societal roles that women hold within the Bedagampana community. In a matrilineal context, where lineage and inheritance are traced through the female line, the prominence of these female figures in folklore underscores the significant place of women in maintaining and transmitting cultural heritage. The roles played by women in these stories mirror their real-life counterparts who actively participate in preserving the community's history and traditions through oral storytelling. This matrilineal influence ensures that women are central to both the social and cultural fabric of the Bedagampana, reflecting their integral role in the continuity and resilience of their traditions.

Another cultural expression of Bedagampana is the practices of exorcism within the community, suggesting a widespread belief in supernatural or spiritual interventions to address perceived instances of possession or spiritual afflictions. These practices may involve rituals, prayers, or ceremonies conducted by religious or spiritual leaders aimed at dispelling malevolent influences or entities. The legendary tales of Male Mahadeshwara Swamy and Sankamma which is one of the most important folklores among Bedagampana also establish the practice of supernatural aspects and exorcism among the Bedagampana for ages. The folklore surrounding Male Mahadeshwara Swamy and Sankamma continues to play a pivotal role in perpetuating the practice of exorcism, as these stories are passed down through generations, reinforcing the community's belief in the supernatural and the power of spiritual intervention. These narratives not only preserve cultural heritage but also provide a framework for understanding and addressing spiritual entities, ensuring the continuity of these traditional practices.

Similarly, totemism is an important part of tribal groups in India. It represents their kinship, and their existence, and distinguishes them from other tribal groups. For the Bedagampana, totems are more than symbolic representations; they are integral to their identity and social structure. These totems, often derived from animals, plants, or natural elements, are believed to embody the spiritual essence of the community's ancestors and serve as protectors. The Indigenous people of Bedagampana like many other tribal groups also depict their kith, kin, and culture with the help of totem.

Besides, like other tribal groups, there is the existence of special celebrations related to agriculture, particularly during seasonal festivals like Ugadi among the Bedagampana. Being an agricultural tribe, these celebrations are crucial as they mark important milestones such as planting, harvesting, and seasonal transitions. The Bedagampana use crops like ragi, til (sesame), rye, foxtail millets, kodo, and corn as their staple foods and include them in special diets during significant occasions like marriages. These agricultural products are deeply integrated into their cultural and ceremonial life. During Ugadi, the Bedagampana prepare traditional dishes using these crops, reflecting their connection to the land and its bounty. These dishes are often shared in community feasts, reinforcing social bonds and celebrating their agricultural heritage. Secondly, they foster community cohesion, bringing people together to celebrate shared traditions and values that often carry spiritual or religious significance, invoking blessings for bountiful harvests and prosperity.

Thus, Bedagampana is highly enriched with its tribal cultural expressions. These expressions encompass rich amalgams of traditions that serve to preserve their history, transmit moral teachings, and uphold spiritual beliefs across generations. Central to their cultural identity are rituals and ceremonies that strengthen social bonds and foster spiritual connections. These practices include offerings to deities and community feasts, which are integral to their social cohesion. Their cultural expressions are derived from values and historical narratives that not only honour their past but also provide a framework for navigating contemporary challenges like their spiritual resilience and cultural continuity.

Rituals and Traditions

The traditions and rituals followed by Bedagampana are unique and consist of various socio-religious accreditations. For example, they have some customized rituals that they observe on Mondays as the day of Lord Shiva. On Mondays, they don't take out cow milk. They save it for the calf. They believe that due to some unavoidable circumstances even if they do so, immediately the bad omens will be seen like their cows will be eaten by the tigers or lions or in some other way the cows will die. Similarly, the Tammadi Bedagampanas who have the right to worship should use only fresh milk as a part of the Puja ritual. They never use milk packets for worship purposes. It is also mandatory not to drink even water before the puja. In case no cow is available to get milk, in such cases they need to go in search of milk without water and food, and once they find the cow they need to take a bath before taking the cow milk out. They also don't practice cultivation or ploughing of land on Mondays, nor do they cut hair and beard on Mondays.

The Puja rituals are one of the most integral parts of their life. This is also important as the worshipping rituals convey the highest similarity between the Bedagampana and the Lingayats. Their worshipping rituals are based on 'Shaiva Paddhati' (Shaivism) where they worship thrice a day regularly. The first puja is done at the dawn 4 am that is also the *Brahma Muhurtam*. The rituals include *Swami Abhishek* which is the bathing of Male Mahadeshwara swami who is the protector of the region. It is followed by *Ashta Pujan* and *Panchabhuta Abhishek* done between morning 10:30 am to 12: 30 pm in the afternoon. The third and final puja is called the *Ishta Trikaal Pujan* done in the evening 6: 30 pm to 8: 30 pm daily. At least 15 Tammadi Bedagampana members join in this worship ritual as priests. They also do special worship on Thursdays. It is also a ritual among the Bedagampana people that they will not offer water, food, or any kind of materialistic things to anyone outside the family on Mondays, which will further help them avoid unnatural calamities.

Except for the major rituals related to daily worship, they also celebrate various other rituals related to different seasons. For example, they do *Bhumi Pujan* or land worship on the next day of Ugadi which is the new year celebrated in South India. Similarly, on the last day when crops are cut during *Sankranti* (the transition of the season), they do a ritual called *Rashi Pujan*. Accordingly, on the last day of the *Kartik* month of the Hindu calendar, they lighten up *Mahajyoti* or sacred flame to eliminate darkness, symbolizing enlightenment and spiritual purity.

The belief systems are also found in their marriage rituals. For example, while going for arranging a marriage between the two families, if they witness any animals like dogs and cats on the way, they believe it is a *Dosha* (bad omen). Similarly, they try to find out the compatibility between the expected bride and groom by breaking the coconut. While breaking the coconut, if it breaks symmetrically without any hurdle, it is believed that the compatibility is good, and the marriage is auspicious. However, if it breaks in an unsymmetrical manner with hurdles, they find it inauspicious and avoid such kinds of marriages. In this age of modernization, the Bedagampana have opened themselves for love marriage and they do the same ritual for such couples also to find out their compatibility and the auspiciousness of the marriage. If the coconut does not break down properly within a single time, in such cases they give a second chance with a new coconut keeping in mind the future and the willingness of the couple. However, if the same happens the second time also, then they ensure not to arrange such love marriages as it is highly inauspicious. These kinds of rituals among Bedagampana are observed in cases of pregnant ladies, childbirth, death, and so on.

The existence of special rituals for pregnant women within the community indicates a widespread cultural practice based on pre-childbirth rituals. These rituals include ceremonies, blessings, or traditions aimed at ensuring the well-being of both the expectant mother and the unborn child, reflecting the cultural significance and importance placed on pregnancy and childbirth within the community. The most commonly mentioned ritual for pregnant women includes *Seemantha* (baby shower), reported by 54.3 percent of respondents. Additionally, *Shastra* (ritual) and *Hossaga* (holy threading) are some other important rituals that are practiced for expectant mothers. The diversity of rituals mentioned reflects the richness of cultural practices surrounding pregnancy within the community.

Similarly, there are various special rituals associated with childbirth within the Bedagampana community. The most prevalent ritual is the naming rituals, mentioned by 61.0 percent of respondents, followed by *Tottilu* (cradle), *Marihabba* (local diety) and *Shastra*. The rituals underscore the cultural significance attached to childbirth within the community.

In the lifecycle of a person, after education, marriage plays a vital role in growing the family and society. Among Bedagampana also marriage plays an important role. All marriages within the Bedagampana occur within the same community. The two sections of Bedagampana i.e. Tammadi and Gowda can marry each other but there is no marital relationship with the Lingayats though they are a vegetarian community and often homogenized with Bedagampana due to some similar cultural practices. Further, this suggests a strong adherence to endogamy, wherein individuals marry within their own social, cultural, or religious group. Endogamous marriages often reinforce social cohesion, preserve cultural identity, and maintain family traditions within the community. Further, like other tribal groups, Bedagampana also practices consanguineous marriage, where individuals marry relatives or members of the same extended family. Consanguineous marriages may reflect cultural or traditional preferences, but they also carry potential health risks associated with genetic disorders.

Due to the confluence with Veerashiava and Lingayats, Bedagampana living in the Male Mahadeshwara Hills restrict their marriage celebrations to two consecutive days, adhering to Shaiva-Paddhati customs. This streamlined approach reflects their adherence to traditional Shaivite rituals and practices, focusing on the essential rites while maintaining spiritual purity and cultural integrity. In contrast, Bedagampana in Tamil Nadu, celebrate their marriage festivities up to five days, accommodating more elaborate ceremonies and community involvement like other tribal groups.

As surveyed, the average age of marriage for girls within the households is 18 years, accounting for 57.1 percent of respondents. Additionally, 36.2 percent reported marrying at the age of 21, while smaller proportions mentioned ages 20 (1.9 percent) and 25 (4.8 percent) as their average age of marriage. These findings suggest the marriages within Bedagampana are as per cultural and legal norms, offering girls maturity while facilitating family formation at a socially acceptable time. These ages often coincide with the completion of education and readiness for familial responsibilities, promoting stability and societal acceptance within the community. The data also indicates the fact that social evils like child marriage are not observed or highly negligible within Bedagampana in recent times.

Besides, there is no prevalence of the dowry system within the Bedagampana. However, it is reported that there is a practice of *Vadhu Dakshina* (bridal dowry). This suggests a widespread cultural tradition where gifts or payments are exchanged from the bride's family to the groom's family as part of the marriage arrangement. This practice contrasts with the dowry system and underscores mutual respect and community ties, reflecting broader cultural norms observed across tribal communities in India. Furthermore, it has been reported that due to the absence of *Vara Dakshina* (bridegroom dowry) or the natural dowry system, there is the absence of inequalities among the Bedagampana, which automatically lessens the social evils like the preference for boy child during childbirth, infanticide, veiling system, etc.

As discussed earlier, the similarity of rituals among Bedagampana, Veerashaivas and Lingayats follows with one significant change. It was the shift in their dietary habits. Under Swamy Male Mahadeshwara's guidance, the Bedagampana community transitioned from a non-vegetarian to a vegetarian diet. This transformation not only altered their lifestyle but also deepened their devotion to Swamy Male Mahadeshwara.

Veerashaiva and Lingayat Communities often stand as a problem for the identities of Bedagampana. However, the field visit during the study observed though there might be some shared elements of marriage rituals within the surveyed community; however, they largely differ from those observed in the Veerashaiva and Lingayat communities. Further, one important factor that differs both communities in terms of marriage is that no marriage is fixed between these two communities though both of them are vegetarian and often merged with each other.

Like marriage, death also plays an important part in the human lifecycle. Especially in the case of religious tribes like Bedagampana, the concept of death is the point to attain salvation and hence plays a crucial role in their rituals and traditions. All households within the Bedagampana practice burial as a death ritual, as it indicates detachment. Only in the case of unnatural deaths like accidents, do they cremate or burn the dead. This suggests a cultural or religious preference for interment as the method of disposing of deceased bodies within the community.

Religion and Spirituality

The Bedagampana's specific ceremonies for pregnancy (e.g., *shreemantha*), childbirth (e.g., naming rituals), marriage (e.g., endogamous practices, *vadhu dakshina* which is common in tribal communities of India but not in practice among Veerashaiva and Lingayat communities, and death (burial practices) are examples of rituals and traditions. These are the specific, repetitive actions and practices that have been handed down through generations. The underlying beliefs that give meaning to these rituals and traditions are rooted in the community's religion and spirituality. For instance, the belief in divine protection during pregnancy or the significance of burial for salvation reflects their spiritual and religious worldview. The endogamous marriage practices and absence of a dowry system are influenced by religious doctrines and cultural values that prioritize social cohesion and respect for traditional norms. While rituals and traditions are the observable practices and customs within a community, religion, and spirituality are the foundational beliefs and values that imbue these practices with meaning and purpose. To observe these foundations, different spiritual practices are observed under different communities like the observation of fast, worship of nature during different seasonal variations, and so on. The Bedagampana indigenous people also practice such spiritual aspects discussed in the following section.

Most of the Bedagampana observe fasting on special days or occasions as a widespread cultural or religious practice, as a form of spiritual observance or as part of traditional rituals. Only a small minority, 3.8 percent, reported not observing fasting on such occasions which may be due to health causes or other external occurrences. The majority of them observe fasts on Mondays, the day of the Lord Shiva, reflecting a prevalent religious or cultural tradition. Additionally, some of them fast on Fridays, while others do so during festivals and on Sundays. This variety underscores the diversity of fasting practices, likely influenced by religious beliefs, cultural customs, and individual preferences within the community.

The most prevalent fasting occasion is *Shivratri*, followed by *Gauri Habba* (Gauri festival) and *Mari Habba* (festival for Goddess). Some of the Bedagampana people also observe fast on Ugadi. These occasions likely hold cultural, religious, or traditional significance, with fasting serving as a form of spiritual observance or as part of ritualistic practices associated with these events.

While discussing the religious and cultural practices, the Bedagampana have their own cultural practices also differentiating them from the Veerashaivas. For example, Bedagampana celebrates Deepavali, the festival of lights, with great gusto. At the time of the Deepavali festival, they offer *Halaravi Seve* (service of the pot of milk). Here they offer 101 pots full of milk to Male Mahadeshwara. The story behind this goes around with Bedagampana's ancestral father Sheshanna Nayaka. There is a prevailing myth that 101 women of Bedagampana offered 101 pots of milk to Male Mahadeshwara who belonged to Sheshanna's family at the time of the Deepavali festival. Hence, it is the religious duty of the members of the family of Sheshanna Nayaka to offer it till now. So, every year, at the time of the festival of Lamps, the members of the Sheshanna Nayaka family, 101 women, with their 101 pots filled with milk, would carry on their heads and go to Male Mahadeshwara temple. They offer puja with that cow milk and the milk used should only be cow milk. There is another belief that if they sell milk during the festival time or if they buy milk for offering puja to Male Mahadeshwara, their cows will give blood instead of giving milk. It is their religious belief. So, they shouldn't buy milk from others or sell the milk to others.

There is another story that Sheshanna Nayaka, a devotee of Male Mahadeshwara, was once carrying a pot of milk to the temple of Male Mahadeshwara. On the way, he felt tired and put down the pot of milk in the middle of the way. He kept it beside his head and slept. When he woke up, he was feeling drowsy and in a drowsy mood, he kicked the pot, unknowingly. The pot fell and the good milk was wasted which was supposed to be offered to Male Mahadeshwara. Male Mahadeshwara sighed the incident in his miraculous vision and got angry with Sheshanna Nayaka. Sheshanna Nayaka's mother also got angry with him. As a result, he could not sustain the anger of his mother, and Male Mahadeshwara. So, he tried to commit suicide. Soon, Male Mahadeshwara appeared in front of him and blessed him with a boon of the wealth of thousands of milking cows. He also told Sheshanna Nayaka to offer 101 pots of milk every year during the festival of lamps, or Deepawali. Bedagampana community is yet respectfully following the duty of offering milk which was assigned by Sheshanna Nayaka. The important fact notable here is that Sheshanna Nayaka is the son of Billayya and Anna Salamma. Billayya and Anna Salamma are a couple. Billayya is the one said to be the first forefather of the Bedagampana tribe.

Other festivals include Navaratri or Dasara Festival, Moni Palu a sect of Bedagampana, observes the *Nandi Kolu Kunitha* ceremony. *Kol* refers to a 25 to 30 foot-long bamboo stick. At the edges of the bamboo stick, they tie cloths of many colours and with brass bangles creating a colourful umbrella. So, holding this Nandi Kol with colourful umbrellas in their hands, they dance in circles in front of the Male Mahadeshwara temple.

The oral stories of Bedagampana also tell us about Rayanna Nayaka who had two daughters. It is said that he is relative of the Chitradurga king Madakari Nayaka. His elder daughter was Devaki, and the younger daughter was Anna Salamma, the mother of Sheshanna Nayaka. His elder daughter Devaki was the daughter-in-law of Alambadi Junje Gowda. It was Alambadi Junje Gowda who built the Male Mahadeshwara temple. He donated 100 acres of land to Male Mahadeshwara fascinated by his miracles. Male Mahadeshwara asked him to build a house for him, which became the temple for his disciples afterward.

When comes to religion and spirituality, some common rituals are shared with the Lingayat community. It includes burying practices followed by food consumption practices and religious beliefs. Bedagampana, Veerashaiva, and the Lingayat communities' exhibit shared devotion to Shiva and adhere to vegetarianism. This mutual reverence for Shiva forms a cornerstone of their religious practices, fostering spiritual connection and identity. Additionally, their commitment to vegetarianism reflects ethical and cultural values centred on non-violence and compassion towards all living beings. While differences may exist in specific rituals and customs, the common ground of devotion to Shiva and vegetarian dietary practices serves as a foundation for common rituals between the two communities, emphasizing shared values.

However, as reported, being a tribal community there are significant differences among Veerashaivas, Lingayats and Bedagampana rituals. Notably, the most important among them is the no intermarriage between the two groups, underscoring distinct social boundaries. Additionally, the differences in the rights of performing puja, suggest varying roles in religious practices. For example, while the Tammadi Bedagampana are the persons who can perform religious rites the Veerashaiva, Lingayats are mainly involved with the responsibility of Mutts like Salur Math, Suttur Math, etc. Further, noted disparities in the process of *lingadharana* also emphasize distinct religious rites and practices between the communities.

These differences likely reflect unique cultural, social, and religious traditions, contributing to the diversity and complexity of their respective identities. *Lingadharana* (wearing of symbol of shiva) plays a special role in it. The *linga* is a symbol that has been adopted by the Bedagampana tribe after they came under the influence of Guru Panditharadhya, Male Mahadeshwara Swamy. The *linga* worn by the Bedagampana is a two-layered sacred stature consisting of the inner layer called *Sthaavar Linga* (the one which is immovable) and the outer layer called *Ishta Linga* (the one which is tangible and can be worshipped). This intricate symbolism of the *linga* signifies the Bedagampana's deep spiritual connection and their unique interpretation of religious doctrines. The *Sthaavar Linga* represents the eternal, unchanging aspect of the divine, anchoring their faith in a stable, immutable reality. In contrast, the *Ishta Linga* embodies the accessible, personal aspect of worship, allowing individuals to engage with their spirituality in a perceivable manner. This dual-layered approach to the *linga* underscores a sophisticated theological understanding that balances tangible and intangible in their spiritual practice. The adoption of the *linga* and its layered symbolism also highlight the Bedagampana's dynamic cultural evolution and adaptability. Influenced by Veerashaivism and Male Mahadeshwar Swamy, their religious practices have been converged and transformed, reflecting a blend of traditional beliefs and new spiritual insights. This synthesis of old and new elements contributes to the Bedagampana's distinct identity, differentiating them from other groups while fostering a sense of unity and continuity within the tribe.

Bedagampana and the Mutt Culture (The Hindu Monastic Institutions)

The Bedagampana tribe, nestled in the hilly regions of Hanur taluka, Karnataka, has a rich cultural heritage deeply intertwined with the Mutt culture, particularly through their long-standing association with Mutts or Hindu monastic institutions. This relationship dates back over six centuries to the arrival of Male Mahadeshwara Swamy, whose settlement among the tribal communities of Soliga and Bedagampana marked the beginning of a spiritual and socio-cultural transformation in the region. The Mutts such as Haradanahalli Mutt, Kunturu Mutt, Suttur Mutt, and Salur Mutt have emerged as prominent centres of religious devotion and community life for the Soliga and Bedagampana tribes. Initially, both tribes participated actively in the religious practices fostered by these Mutts. However, over time, a divergence occurred due to differing dietary practices. The Soliga, traditionally non-vegetarian, gradually distanced themselves from the Mutt culture, while the Bedagampana, adopted a vegetarian diet, deepening their commitment and involvement with the Mutts.

For the Bedagampana community, the Mutt is not merely a place of worship but a central institution where their religious and community identities are nurtured and sustained. They play integral roles within these institutions, serving as priests and actively participating in the administration and rituals of the Mutts. This involvement underscores their dedication to preserving and perpetuating their cultural heritage through religious practices and community activities. The presence of Male Mahadeshwara Swamy, who settled among the Bedagampana and Soliga communities, initiated a process of cultural exchange and mutual enrichment. The Mutts became focal points not only for spiritual guidance but also for social cohesion and development within these tribal communities. Over time, the Bedagampana have integrated the teachings and practices of the Mutt into their daily lives, forming a distinctive cultural mosaic that blends traditional tribal customs with Hindu religious traditions.

The role of the Mutts in Bedagampana society extends beyond religious functions; they serve as educational centres, imparting knowledge of scriptures, philosophy, and practical skills necessary for community life. This educational aspect has empowered generations of Bedagampana to uphold their traditions while adapting to changing social and economic landscapes. Economically, the Mutts often support the community through various welfare activities, including healthcare, education scholarships, and agricultural initiatives. These efforts not only enhance the well-being of the Bedagampana but also reinforce the symbiotic relationship between the Mutts and the local community. Despite modern influences and challenges, the Bedagampana continue to cherish and safeguard their connection with the Mutt culture. Their dedication to vegetarianism as a religious practice further underscores their commitment to the principles and teachings espoused by the Mutts. This steadfast adherence to tradition, coupled with their openness to change, has enabled the Bedagampana to navigate the complexities of modernity while preserving the essence of their cultural identity.

In contemporary times, a significant challenge arises as Mutts serve as crucial hubs where diverse cultures assimilate. This cultural amalgamation has led to the Bedagampana often being conflated with the Veerashaiva and Lingayats. Despite their distinct traditions and practices, the Bedagampana face the risk of cultural homogenization within broader societal perceptions. This merging can obscure their unique identity and spiritual heritage nurtured through centuries of affiliation with Mutts, highlighting the complexities of cultural preservation amidst evolving social dynamics. However, despite such challenges, the enduring association of Bedagampana tribe with the Mutt culture exemplifies a profound intertwining of spiritual beliefs, cultural practices, and community cohesion. Through their sustained engagement with the Mutts, they have not only preserved their heritage but also enriched it, ensuring that future generations inherit a legacy of faith, resilience, and community harmony.

Bedagampana and the Veerashaiva Lingayats

Male Mahadeshwara, the picturesque hilly region is enriched with its vibrant cultural landscape. In the heart of it lie two distinct communities, the Bedagampana and the Soligas. While the Soligas are identified as Scheduled tribe under the Indian Scheduled list, their close neighbours Bedagampana still strives for their identity. According to the reports of The Hindu, April 05, 2021, there are almost 31,500 Bedagampana living in Chamrajnagar of Karnataka and a few in the border areas like Erode district of Tamil Nadu. Still in the social category list drawn out by the state government, the existence of Bedagampana is not found. This tribal community is merged with Veerashaiva Lingayat which is put under the category III (B) of the backward community list of the state.

This convergence has mostly occurred for performing puja and daily rituals of Male Mahadeshwar which is in a dense forest, the Lingayat seers found it difficult to attend and thought of Bedagampana tribals who can perform the rituals on their behalf. So, they were converted to Lingayats, and for this, the shifting arrangements were made. It relates to the history of 12th century Anubhava Mantapa, where Basaveshwara, the father of Lingayatism, merely tied a *linga* in a piece of cloth on the neck of a barber, hunter, sweeper, shoemaker, courtesan and declared them as *Sharana* meaning saints. But those – 'Hadapad Apanna' (the barber) continued his profession of hair cutting, 'Sule Sankavve' (the courtesan) lived in her profession of prostitution, 'Haralayya' (the cobbler) continued his shoemaking work. Hence historically, the Lingayat Movement has adopted the symbolic and emotional way of converting the marginal people into the Veerashaiva religion. So, potters, carpenters, blacksmiths, and washermen, who were in a lower stratum of the social hierarchy, have been identified as *Sharana*, who will lose their caste identity and treated equally in 'Anubhava Mantapa' (chair of experience) which was established by Basaveshwara. But these saints after becoming *Sharana* also continued their professions. The list includes 'Aydakki Marayya (a barber), 'Dohara Kakkayya' (a tanner), 'Ambigara Chowdaiah' (a boatman), 'Madara Chennaiah' (a cobbler), 'Devara Dasimayya' (a weaver), and 'Talawar Kamideva' (a village watchman), who continued their profession. Maintaining personal hygiene, worship, writing of *vachanas* (poetry or verses), and participating in Anubhava Mantap, these marginalized saints continued debating and discussing along with their respective professions.

Further, to understand the scenario one has to go through the etymology and chronology of the Bedagampana. The word 'Beda' refers to hunter, whereas the word 'Gam' indicates tribal, and 'Pana' refers to community. Hence, the word 'Bedagampana' means hunting tribal community. The similar tribal groups like Beda, Berad or Bedara are listed as tribes in the Indian Scheduled Tribes lists. Further, the tribal histories are oral and not documented in most of the cases. The same goes for Bedagampana which is enriched with various types of oral histories. One of the major oralities related with Bedagampana is with the hunter named Bedara Kannappa who is said to be the reincarnation of Arjuna. In Mahabharata, a fight between Lord Shiva and Arjuna is referred in which pleased by Arjuna's devotion Lord Shiva offers him Pashupat Astra. He also blesses him to be reincarnated as a hunter called Bedara Kannappa in Kali Yuga who is further said to be the forefather of the Bedagampana. The temple of Hunter Bedara Kannappa, the Shaiva devotee, is still located in the Srikalahasti of Andhra Pradesh. It is important in the reference that histories suggest almost 600 years ago, the ancestors of Bedagampana lived in Srikalahasti who later migrated to Karnataka due to a royal marriage alliance.

To move ahead, the chronology goes further to 15th century when Male Mahadeshwara Swamy who is said to be the protector of seven hills of Mahadeshwara Betta arrived at this region to take out the people residing there from deprivation. As mentioned earlier, he had two devotees who were the brothers, Karayya and Billayya. While the Karayya is said to be the great forefather of the tribal group Soliga, similarly Billayya was the forefather of the Bedagampana. When they came into contact with Male Mahadeshwara Swamy, they were taught about the righteous things and Swamiji further advised them to leave hunting as it is immoral to take life of living beings. The family of Billayya readily agreed to it but as the area was mainly a hilly region and agriculture was difficult there hence Karayya's family decided to retain hunting as their main occupation and remained non-vegetarian. Under the devotion of Male Mahadeshwara Billayya and his family became vegetarian and wore *linga* as their symbol. Thus, Bedagampana since then left hunting and became vegetarian while Soligas remained non-vegetarian. This is also a major reason why no marriage alliance between Soliga and Bedagampana is done though they are akin neighbour or distinct brothers. They started to wear *linga* and refer to themselves as 'Bedagampana Lingayat' which is always merged with 'Veerashaiva Lingayats' of Category III (B).

The situation here is very complicated as though held from a tribal genesis due to this convergence with the Veerashaiva Lingayats they don't exist as Bedagampana in any caste/tribe list of the country. Various commissions have also been constituted in this regard like the Kantharaj commission of 2015, however, every time the Bedagampana lose their rights from being a tribe mainly due to three particular reasons: (i) there is no socio-religious/cultural inequality/untouchability observed among them; (ii) being a tribe they cannot be vegetarian and (iii) they wear *linga* which is similar to the customs of Lingayats. Nevertheless, if moved chronologically, the reasons behind all these factors can be understood easily. While the major reasons behind being a vegetarian and wearing *linga* have been discussed above, the observation of inequality or untouchability is not a criterion for referring tribes.

In real terms, none of the tribal communities of the country practices any kind of untouchability among them. The case of untouchability is related to the 'Scheduled Castes' as per the Press Information Bureau, Government of India. Ministry of Social Justice & Empowerment, 24 February 2015. On the other hand, Scheduled Tribes are completely different from the above clause. Though there is no particular definition of tribes in the constitution, Article 342 accepts Census 1931 as its base to understand Schedule tribes i.e. 'backward tribes' living in the 'excluded' and 'partially excluded' areas. In this reference, it becomes important to understand the definitions of 'excluded' and 'partially excluded' areas. The report presented by the Thakkar Committee,1947, which constituted some of the pioneers of tribal rights in India including Jaipal Singh Munda, defined 'the excluded and partially excluded areas are well-defined areas populated either predominantly or to a considerable extent by aboriginals.' Though it also clarifies that, 'the excluded and partially excluded areas, however, do not by any means cover the entire population of tribal origin, and in many cases represent only a comparatively small proportion of the aboriginal population, the rest of them being scattered over non-excluded areas', many areas like South Kanara of then Madras province was kept under excluded areas based on 'inaccessibility of these areas is largely responsible for their exclusion as well as for the for the backward conditions of their inhabitants.'

Further, they were first represented under the Government of India Act of 1935 in provincial assemblies. If the historical, geographical, and contemporary living conditions of Bedagampana are taken into consideration, then it can be observed that even after the 77 years of independence the Bedagampana lives in extremely poor condition even without basic amenities like electricity, water, and transport. Their geographical access is very much limited being in the Male Mahadeshwar Hills of Chamrajnagara which is a part of South Canara of then Madras presidency. Their backwardness and geographical isolation are factors that qualify them for being a 'Scheduled Tribe' like their ancestral brother Soligas.

After independence, the Lokur Committee (1965) established five criteria for the identification of tribes based on primitive traits, distinct culture, geographical isolation, shyness of contact with the community at large, and backwardness. Dhebar Commission (1960–61) identified, 'the inaccessibility of the area; exclusiveness and distinctive way of life of the tribal population; marked disparity in economic standards in relation to the people of the surrounding area; marked disparity in the level of education; Stage of advancement and degree of assimilation; Comparative development of non-tribal population to the tribal population; and Relative development of the State to the development of the area in which there is concentration of the tribal population' as the measure to recognize a scheduled area.

Similarly, the Kunwar committee (2006) takes up the reference of Article 338 and Article 338 (A) of the constitution as its base stating,

> the framers of the Constitution took note of the fact that certain communities in the country were suffering from extreme social, educational and economic backwardness arising out of age-old practice of untouchability and certain others on account of the primitive agricultural practices, lack of infrastructure facilities and geographical isolation, and, therefore, these communities needed special consideration for safeguarding their interests and for their accelerated socio-economic development. These communities were notified as Scheduled Castes and Scheduled Tribes as per provisions contained in Clause 1 of Articles 341 and 342 of the Constitution of India respectively.

Bhuria Committee (2002–2004) defines tribes as:

> Their human development indices (having economic and social components) are the lowest as compared to any other section of the people. Land and forests are the two basic resources of the tribal life-support system. There have been assaults on both.

The fact notable here is that 'agricultural and forest produces' are the life-support system for the Bedagampana living in the remotest part of the Male Mahadeshwara Hills as stated by the above committee. Further, most of their inhabitation regions come under the Forest Rights Act of 2006 and displacement and rehabilitation are noticeable phenomena here. For example, according to various news reports after the ban on cattle rearing in the forest the Bedagampana living in the forest, especially near the Bargur region have faced many livelihood challenges due to the destruction of dairy farming.

The most important and recent report submitted by the National Scheduled Tribes Commission is the Virginius Xaxa report (2014) which is taken as a milestone in redefining the tribes and their issues. It is the first of its kind report that elaborates on the meaning of tribe in detail and columns a separate section for defining the tribes. Xaxa Committee (2014) urges,

> It is necessary to examine the early origins of the concept of 'tribe' and its transformation in various historical and political contexts, specifically during the colonial period in the Indian sub-continent.

It talks about the varying theory of Indo-Western concepts of tribe, where the Indian views,

CULTURAL PRACTICES AND BELIEFS

An amalgam of the various traits ascribed to tribal groups include relative egalitarianism within the absence of complex political structures, strong and functional kinship bonds, cooperation, territorial integrity, cultural and linguistic distinctiveness, and lower levels of technology. In the case of the latter view, tribes are seen as 'primitive' societies in the sense of lacking all the traits of modern, Western society in that they are non-literate, 'uncivilised', non-industrial, rural, and so on.

The report also discusses the changing trajectories of tribes based on religious practices and quotes,

> In the 1901 census, tribes were identified as those who 'practiced animism' thus placing religious practices at the center. Therefore, those practicing Hinduism were viewed as castes, while those practicing animism were labelled tribes, although this criterion would change in the following decades such that, at present, Scheduled Tribes can practice any religion, including Hinduism and Christianity.

Thus, the recent report of the Xaxa committee rejects the concept of identification of tribes based on religion. Thus, the nature-worshipping Bedagampana who due to convergence with 'Veerashaiva Lingayats' have adopted Shaiva rituals as a part of their religious belief can practice any religion yet can be declared tribe based on their historical, physiographical nature and socio-economic solitary. It is also supported by the Kaka Kalelkar Commission which is also the first Backward Classes Commission under Article 340 argued that the tribes:

> lead a separate exclusive existence and are not fully assimilated in the main body of the people. Scheduled Tribes may belong to any religion. They are listed as Scheduled Tribes, because of the kind of life led by them, (Xaxa Report, 2014).

All the above criterion indicates the fact that the tribal communities are based more on their geographical and living conditions rather than socio-cultural inequalities. Besides, the recent Task Force led by Hrusikesh Panda created under the aegis of the Ministry of Tribal Affairs in 2014 has formulated some new criteria based on the factors,

> Socio-economic, including educational, backwardness, Historical geographical isolation which may or may not exist today; Distinct language/dialect; Presence of a core culture relating to life-cycle, marriage, songs, dance, paintings, folklore; and Endogamy, or in case of exogamy, marital relationship primarily with other STs (The Hindu, January 12, 2023).

Bedagampana as a tribal group fit under all these criteria. For example, the Bedagampanas are residents of isolated hilly terrain which difficult to access geographically. They have their own tribal cultural aspects like burying the dead, giving *vadhu dakshi*na in marriage, widow remarriage, etc. as a part of their ceremonial features. Similarly, the Bedagampana celebrates and worships nature like other nature worshipping tribes. For example, in their marriages, they take *pheras* which is also called as *saptapadis* of different plants like bamboo instead of fire-pit. They even don't see the Arundhati star which is seen in the Lingayat marriages. Accordingly, they have traditional medicinal practitioners who are dependent on forest and tree produce for healing aspects of diseases like jaundice, piles or snake bites. All these factors establish Bedagampana as a tribe. Further, the fact that there is no give and take policy between Lingayats and Bedagampana distinguishes the two communities from each other. No marriage is done among them. Most of their marriages are endogamy in nature. Further, the Lingayats are often linked with Male Mahadeshwar who came originally from the Srisailam region to Karnataka with whom the present-day followers of Lingayats migrated to the region of Chamrajnagar. It is important in this regard that the Soliga and the Bedagampana were indigenous to this place which distinguishes them from the Lingayat community at large. There is a huge difference in the process of *Linga dharana* between Lingayats and Bedagampana. According to the book *Lingayat Dharma (Veerashaiva Religion)* by Munavalli (2007), the Lingayats have six major rites i.e.

> (1) lingadharana (wearing of the linga),
>
> (2) lingadiksha,
>
> (3) isthalinga worship,
>
> (4) namakarana (christening or naming ceremony),
>
> (5) marriage and
>
> (6) lingaikya (death).
>
> Lingadharana means wearing of the linga. The family priest gives the linga to the baby before its birth (usually during the eighth month of pregnancy) or after the baby is born. It is noteworthy that the baby, while in the mother's womb, can receive the linga through its mother. This linga is worn until the child is 10 ~ 12 years old, at which time the child is considered fit to receive religious instructions and the isthalinga from a religiously ordained Guru.

Due to the arrangements by sheers of Lingayat Mutts during the times of Male Mahadeshwar Swamy, though all these rites play an important role among the Bedagampana tribal group also, yet there is significant variation in the process of this *Linga dharana*. While, as mentioned above, the Lingayats starts *lingadharana* at the age of 10–12 years by a guru which is also known as *lingadiksha*, the Bedagampana wears this *linga* since they are born and no such ritual of *lingadiksha* is observed by the Bedagampana. These cultural distinctions underscore the Bedagampana's unique tribal identity, separate from the Lingayats, highlighting their traditional practices and ceremonies. Besides, religious rites also various socio-infrastructural factors ensure the assertion of Bedagampana in the Scheduled tribe list.

A crucial point here is that the hills of Male Mahadeshwara where the Bedagampana live are highly remote, backward, and unreachable. The transport facility is a dire need of the community. The only primary health centre (PHC) is located in the foothill which is approximately 30 km from the inner Bettas (hills). They need to walk up to such long distances if they want to come for health checkups or market facilities or wait for heavy vehicles which is very rare, and hence in most cases, they need to walk through hilly and rocky terrain for their day-to-day needs. The major disease found among the Bedagampana is the presence of anaemia. Almost 15 percent patients of recorded in the health centre are affected by it. In India, the problem of anaemia especially sickle cell anaemia, thalassemia are mainly found among tribal societies. As there is a lack of sickle cell test measures in the health centre of Male Mahadeshwar Hills, hence it is not sure whether the patients are suffering especially from sickle cell or not. But as anaemia is highly found here hence there is a high probability of sickle cell disease which needs to be identified.

Among all these various issues like land relocation due to forest acts have also been faced by Bedagampana. As per a report of Times of India (June 29, 2020) a comprehensive plan to relocate over 225 families from Changadi village of Chamrajnagar district have been done by government. Even forty-four families of Bedagampana tribes living in Thokkere and two in Medagalane, along with 26 Soliga families, have voluntarily come forward for relocation due to the lack of basic infrastructure like road, hospitals, schools etc. It is to be noted here that Govt Girijana Ashrama School which is a co-educational school located in the Hanur block of Chamarajanagara district in Karnataka provides residential education to tribal students in the area. The Soliga tribal students are part of this school but due to the lack of identity crisis the Bedagampana are deprived of it.

The members of Bedagampana community have claimed for inclusion in the Scheduled Tribes list based on the criteria that establish themselves as tribe. They have also rejected the fact that they have no relation with Veerashaiva Lingayat which is completely different sect but due to their acceptance of *linga* followed by their ancestors they are always put into the category III (B) of Veerashaiva Lingayat by the caste census officials. They have also raised the issue to the former Minister of Tribal Affairs regarding the issue but due to the non-intervention of state delegates, the case was neglected at the Central level. As a result, they are deprived

CHAPTER 4

of various government schemes like PM JANMAN yojana, ashram schools etc. Further, the availability of roads and transportation facility is their basic need.

Summary

The Bedagampana community stands as a testament to the rich cultural diversity and resilience of indigenous tribes in India. Despite their unique cultural expressions, deep-rooted traditions, and distinct religious practices, they face significant challenges in gaining recognition and support as a Scheduled Tribe. The interplay between their rituals, traditions, and spiritual beliefs forms the backbone of their cultural identity, highlighting their profound connection to their heritage and the natural world.

Their vibrant folklore, community rituals, and endogamous practices underscore the importance they place on preserving their cultural identity and social cohesion. These traditions not only reinforce their community bonds but also serve as a living archive of their history and values. However, the Bedagampana's struggle for recognition is compounded by their historical and cultural associations with the Lingayat community. This association has led to their marginalization and exclusion from the official Scheduled Tribes list, depriving them of essential benefits and support. The complexities of their identity, influenced by historical migrations and socio-religious transformations, necessitate an acute understanding and acknowledgment of their unique status.

In addressing the challenges faced by the Bedagampana, it is crucial to recognize and validate their distinct cultural and religious identity. Ensuring their inclusion in the Scheduled Tribes list would not only provide them with much-needed support but also affirm their place in the diverse cultural mosaic of India. As the Bedagampana continue to navigate the complexities of modernity and tradition, their rich heritage and resilient spirit remain a powerful testament to their enduring legacy

India is a country of various castes, creeds, and tribe. Yet various unrecognized tribes like Bedagampana do not even exist in any document. They are deprived of the basic facilities, and requirements to live a life. Hence, the time has come to take out these vulnerable communities from the path of destruction and cultural extinction. The Bedagampana are a vibrant example of this and if recognized as a tribe they will indeed be the very first vegetarian tribe of the country. The next chapter therefore concentrates on the status of education, health, and infrastructure facilities among the Bedagampana tribe to understand their contemporary requirements.

CHAPTER 5

Education, Health, and Infrastructure

Introduction

India as a developing country is moving fast towards IT sectors, quality education, smart cities, world-class roads, fast rails, nutritional food, high-end research, etc. The lifestyle of people is changing continuously through the adoption of a world-class knowledge sector, research, and scientific innovations. However, in between all of these, the indigenous people of India are still under tremendous pressure to get their basic necessities.

2011 census says that more than 10 crore tribals are there in Indian states. The women ratio is 990/1000 males which is better than many mainstream societies. But still, the literacy rate among these people is 59 percent. The malnutrition rate among tribals is 39.5 percent according to National Family Health Survey (NFHS-5) 2019–21. One in every 86 births among tribals is suffering from Sickle Cell Disease (SCD) as estimated by ICMR, the number of thalassemia varies from 11 to 71 percent among tribal groups depending on regions, according to World Malaria Report 2021, in 2021, over 90 percent of India's 161,516 documented malaria cases were concentrated in only eight states, all of which had large tribal populations. According to the Ministry of Health and Family Welfare, the infant mortality rate (IMR) in Scheduled Tribes is 50.3 as of 2019–21 who died at the birth level. All these problems indicate the lack of basic infrastructure to live a healthy and prosperous life. Further, the lack of basic amenities is creating a new world of suffering, negligence, carelessness, and acute poverty. Problems of roads, schools, health land, and tribal harassment by either the forest department, police department, or revenue department are some common occurrences that the tribes face in their day-to-day life.

There will be several cases where no records of tribal lands are found along with tempering of land records by the government officials, or their rights will be bypassed for political gains or pressure from mainstream societies. Approximately proposals for 40 communities are pending which seeks ST status. In many cases, their basic documents are not even provided either due to the lack of interest by authorities or due to the lack of knowledge by the tribal people. Various instances can be found where there is a lack of power supply in tribal areas and for the basic necessities of life also, they need to struggle every time. This involves tribal hamlets or their domestic animals like cows falling into the grip of wild animals like tigers, lions, and so on. These problems are further extended where in the name of caste, creed, religion, and superstitions, these forest-dwelling tribals often become prey to social evils like illegal conversion of religions.

Resettlement and Rehabilitation due to many development-induced displacements are also common phenomena among the tribes. Violation of the fifth and sixth schedules of the Indian constitution that talks about PESA Act (1996) in the name of a welfare scheme, the building of bypass roads and national highways through houses, lands, hills, or green fields of tribal people are nothing new. Sometimes this displacement happens due to natural calamities like floods, and cyclones. Besides, there are numerous examples where the school-going children of the tribes report various health problems due to poor infrastructural facilities like toilets, water problems causing jaundice, cholera etc., and improper sewage systems that cause vectorial diseases like malaria, dengue etc. Similarly, malnutrition, underweight children, and pregnant women suffering from anaemia are pathetic in various tribal regions.

This section of the book tries to find out the condition of education, health, and the status of other social infrastructure of Bedagampana tribal groups. It will also discuss about the assistance from the government and their benefits among these group in the following sections.

Education Systems

Education is the weapon to ignite the proper cultivation of the mind. It teaches the way of life, to live life, and to fight for social justice, liberty, and rights. It is a path toward growth and perhaps the only element that differentiates a human being from other living organisms. The world is going through an 87 percent literacy rate (World Bank, 2021). Among them, while developed nations have already achieved approximately 99 percent of literacy rate, the ratio in developing and under-developed countries is relatively less i.e., 70 percent on average. In the case of India, the literacy rate is 74.04 percent (Census of India, 2011) and as per the latest report released by the National Survey of

India, 2022, it is 77.7 percent. But when it comes to the tribal population, the figures are comparatively low which is 59 percent among them 68.40 percent are male whereas 49.40 percent are females (Census of India, 2011). According to the data availed in 2015, the overall dropout rates are respectively 31.3 percent for primary education i.e. I - V, 48.2 percent for standard I – VIII, and 62.4 percent for the classes I - X. If analyzed acutely it can be observed that the drop rates increase at the higher educational standards. The data encourages us to understand the reasons behind the dropout rates in schools among tribal youths and the challenges they face in their day-to-day life in pursuing formal education. Further, it becomes important to understand the status of education among the Bedagampana tribal group.

Educational Details

The responses gathered during the survey are distributed across eight categories representing different levels of education. The largest group is PUC (Pre-University Course), comprising 27.6 percent of respondents, followed closely by those respondents who have attended classes up to 8 to 10 (24.8 percent). The number of respondents also vary in the categories of 'uneducated' (7.6 percent) to those holding post-graduate degrees (1.9 percent). Intermediate categories like those who reached up to classes 6 to 7 (13.3 percent) and classes 1 to 5 (17.1 percent) show moderate representation. Thus, a diverse educational background among respondents is found with significant representation in mid-level categories such as PUC and attending classes till 8 to 10. While higher education levels (degree and PG) are less common, they still represent a notable portion of the sample. The presence of respondents categorized as uneducated or at the primary level of education ('Anganwadi') highlights the inclusivity of the sample across educational spectra.

School Dropouts in Family

The data on school dropouts within families reveals that only 11.4 percent reported having school dropouts, while a significant majority of 88.6 percent did not experience any dropouts indicating that school dropout rates are relatively low among the surveyed population. This suggests a high level of school retention within these families, with nearly nine out of ten families ensuring their children continue their education. The dropouts are mainly after high school as there is a lack of schools in the region and transportation facilities are also very poor which makes most of the students leave their schooling after class 8. An interesting fact here is that the reasons behind the dropout of boys and girls vary indicating a need to understand social barriers regarding this.

CHAPTER 5

Dropout Reason for Boys

The data on dropout reasons for boys reveals significant insights into the barriers to education within the surveyed population. 88.6 percent of boy children dropped out due to a lack of transport facilities. This overwhelming percentage indicates a critical infrastructure gap, where inadequate or non-existent transport options severely hinder access to education. The consequence of this is far-reaching, potentially limiting boys' future opportunities, reducing their employability, and perpetuating cycles of poverty and under-education in these communities. Additionally, 6.7 percent dropped out because there were no high school facilities available nearby. These points to an acute need for more schools or educational institutions in certain areas. The impact of this lack is profound, as it denies children their right to education and the associated benefits of literacy, critical thinking, and personal development. Family problems were cited by 4.7 percent as the reason for school dropouts. While this is the least reported cause, it still represents a significant social issue. Family-related challenges, such as financial instability, domestic issues, or health problems, can disrupt a child's educational journey. The impact here is multifaceted, affecting not only the child's education but also their emotional and psychological well-being. Cumulatively, these dropout reasons emphasize the urgent need for targeted interventions. Addressing the transportation barrier would have the most significant impact, potentially reducing the dropout rate by nearly 90 percent. Moreover, increasing the number of accessible schools and providing support for families facing difficulties could further mitigate dropout rates. The consequences of inaction are stark: continued educational deprivation, limited economic mobility, and ongoing social inequities. Therefore, comprehensive strategies involving infrastructure development, educational facility expansion, and family support services are crucial to ensuring benefits from continuous education.

Dropout Reason for Girls

The primary survey states that the major issue is a lack of transport facilities for the girls also which indicates a high need for transportation facilities in the area. While for girls, additionally, poor family background and lack of interest are also notable factors. The leading cause, affecting 49.5 percent is lack of transport facilities. The impact remains critical, hindering access to education and prospects for the girl child. Further, family background and economic hardships as a barrier underscores the need for financial support and social interventions to ensure girls can continue their education. 27.6 percent of the respondents suggest motivational or engagement issues. This could reflect deeper societal attitudes toward girls' education, requiring efforts to foster interest and demonstrate the value of education. Failure to address these issues will continue to limit educational access and perpetuate social and economic inequalities for both boys and girls. Comprehensive interventions tailored to the specific needs of each gender are essential for reducing dropout rates and ensuring equitable educational opportunities.

Case Studies

Discussing case studies is crucial for understanding Bedagampana because they provide detailed, context-specific insights into the unique challenges and dynamics of the area. By examining individual schools and their circumstances, case studies reveal the particular needs and resource gaps that might not be apparent through broader surveys or statistical data alone. Each village or school in Bedagampana has its own cultural, social, and economic context. Case studies allow for a deeper understanding of how these factors influence educational outcomes and student behaviour, including dropout rates. This can inform future policy and intervention designs tailored to Bedagampana's specific needs. The study focuses on four village schools and the sole high school in the M. M. Hills region, aiming to gain insights into the local educational system. By examining these case studies, the research seeks to identify the specific needs of these institutions and understand the underlying causes of student dropouts in the area. The findings will provide a comprehensive overview of the challenges faced by these schools and highlight potential areas for intervention and improvement.

Case Study 1: Anganwadi School, Shantinagar

The Anganwadi school consists of 20 students out of which the majority belong to Bedagampana. The school is important as almost 500 Tammadi people of Bedagampana priests reside surrounding the school. The school had only one teacher who also belonged to the Tammadi group of Bedagampana along with an assistant. While the teacher gets the regular salary as a part of her occupation, there is no provision of salary for the assistant and hence the assistant is paid some remuneration by the teacher herself. The school does not provide any free books, uniforms, or any other material as an assistance to the kids. The children were taught basic numeric, Kannada as well as English language as a part of its curriculum. The school has a system to provide small snacks to the students like Ragi laddoos. Further infrastructural facilities like electricity, water, and toilets were available. Eggs or any non-vegetarian food is completely prohibited, as they believe it brings bad omens or if some children taste it under the influence of other tribal locals, then the snakes will disturb them. Hence, the school also does not offer any kind of non-vegetarian food to any of the students concerning the religious beliefs of the Bedagampana. Thus, it can be said that socio-religious beliefs play an important role in the society as well as in the dietary practices of Bedagampana.

Case Study 2: Government Higher Primary School, Gorasane, Male Mahadeshwara Hills

The school consists of classes from 1st to 7th standard. Most of the students who study here shift to the school run by Salur Mutt after 7th standard. This school consists of 90 Bedagampana and 40 Soliga students. There is a provision of meals for the students under Poshan Shakti Yojana run by the government under which food items like bananas, milk, and eggs are recommended to serve. But due to the Bedagampana students, the school authorities cook separately a pure vegetarian meal and also they have stopped providing eggs in the meal. For the cordial relationship between the Bedagampana and Soliga communities, both of the communities have agreed on this food menu due to which instead of eggs bananas, groundnuts, etc. are provided for complete nutrition. The school is being supported under CSR programs run by IndiaMart Inter NESH Ltd. who provide school kits like bags, pens, pencils, etc. in June every year. Besides, some donors also donate equipment like computers for the students. The school is not covered under Samagra Shiksha Abhiyan yet and the Bedagampana children are provided OBC scholarship, as they are not declared as a tribe. It was also reported that the cost for the mid-day meal provided is as per 70 rs per day which is insufficient due to which most of the time the teachers pay the extra amounts on their own. Similarly, for the welfare of the school, Wi-Fi has been connected by the contribution of 17,000 rupees by the teachers. The school consists of seven teachers, and 3 assistants as cooks. The seven teachers include 1 Principal, 1 Physical Education Teacher, 3 permanent teachers, and 2 guest teachers. The school was developed in terms of Infrastructure like computer lab, proper toilet facilities etc, most of which are contributed by the CSR activities.

Case Study 3: Government High School, Tholasikere

The school was established in the year 1994. The school also consists of classes from 1st to 7th standard. Approximately 58 Bedagampana students study here. The authorities informed that assistance like books, food, and uniforms are provided freely to the students but due to lack of transport facilities, most of the students drop out of education after the completion of 7th standard. The school has only one permanent teacher along with a guest teacher who has been teaching in the school for the last 12 years. The service of the guest teacher is counted from the March session. Facilities like mid- day meals as well as toilets are available but the facility of water through 'Jal Jeevan Yojana' is not successful; though pipelines are there, no water is discharged from those pipelines. Hence wells and borewells established under CSR activities are the source of water for them. An Anganwadi school is also there attached to the high school.

Case Study 4: Government High School, Indiganatha

This school was mainly dominated by Bedagampana students as out of 47 students studying there 46 students were of Bedagampana while only one of them belonged to the Soliga tribe. The school consists of 1 principal, 2 guest teachers, and one assistant. Facilities of the toilet, mid-day meal, etc. are available but no electricity and no water facility is there which is a major problem for the entire area.

Case Study 5: Veda Agama Sanskrit School- The Mutt School

This is a school run by the prestigious Salur Mutt of Male Mahadeshwara Hills which runs classes from 6th to 10th standard and is the only school providing opportunities for high school in the area. The school was established in the year 1969 which provide free education to all, where they also teach Veda and Sanskrit as a special subject. All the students in this school belong to the Bedagampana community where 125 students are enrolled for Veda learning whereas other 375 students are enrolled in Sanskrit education. The teachers teaching in the school belong to both Bedagampana as well as Lingayat communities. As per the data received, the dropout rate in the school is approximately 22–25 percent which is mainly due to the lack of transportation facilities. In the last Pre- University Course– PUC (12th standard) 45 passed-out Bedagampana students completed the PUC examination successfully. The school also encourages education by preventing social evils like child marriage. For example, it was noticed that in recent years 28–30 child marriages have been registered within the region but due to the intervention of the Mutt school and Swamiji, those children were encouraged to get educated first and hence enrolled in the school. Further, it has been claimed by the school that a cent percent of students passed the high school examination, and due to the support and assistance provided by the school approximately, 60 percent of the students choose higher education as a part of their step ahead. They provide financial assistance of rupees 5000 for the lower classes whereas a sum of rupees 7500 is being provided to the students of higher classes. They also provide educational kits like uniforms, bags, books, and other needed materials freely. As reported, though most of the passed-out students get enrolled in basic courses like humanities and social sciences at the graduation level yet there is a high demand for professional courses like vocational education, nursing, etc. in the region. Hence, opening higher educational institutions (HEIs) in vocational courses in the region can meet the needs of the local Bedagampana people.

Summary

The case studies and data from the Male Mahadeshwar Hills region paint a clear picture of the critical challenges faced by students, particularly due to the lack of transport facilities. This major issue significantly contributes to the high dropout rates among students, despite the provision of supportive measures such as mid-day meals in all schools. Meals like Anna-Sambar, Bissi Belle Bath, and other nutritious options are provided freely during lunchtime, ensuring that students receive at least one wholesome meal a day. However, food scarcity is not a primary concern for these tribal communities, as they can often access food from the jungle and agricultural fields.

Corporate Social Responsibility (CSR) activities have been initiated for the educational development of these villages by corporate companies like ICICI. Nevertheless, the problem of high dropout rates persists, especially after students complete the 7th standard. The main barrier is the distance to higher education institutions like the Mutt school, compounded by the absence of reliable transport facilities. The few available jeep drivers prefer to cater to more lucrative customers from outside the region, who can afford to pay 200–250 rupees per trip. This economic preference leaves local students stranded, unable to commute to schools that offer higher education.

If daily bus services were established, it would significantly alleviate this issue, providing students with the means to reach Male Mahadeshwar Hills for further education. The community has expressed a clear demand for such services, recognizing the potential impact on improving educational outcomes. Additionally, there is a strong desire for job-oriented education and the establishment of professional educational centres within closer proximity. The nearest skill education centre is in Chamrajnagar, a daunting 110 kilometres away, making it inaccessible for most students.

Despite these logistical hurdles, the enthusiasm for education among the Bedagampana tribe remains high. Students are keenly interested in pursuing higher education, and there is substantial awareness about its importance. However, the lack of government assistance and inadequate transport infrastructure significantly hinder their educational progress. This situation calls for urgent intervention to provide better transport solutions and closer educational facilities. Improving transport infrastructure would not only reduce dropout rates but also empower students to pursue their educational aspirations. Government and community initiatives could focus on creating reliable and affordable transport options, such as daily bus services or subsidized transport for students. Additionally, establishing satellite centres for higher education and vocational training within the region could provide more accessible opportunities for skill development and job readiness.

In conclusion, addressing the transport challenges in the Male Mahadeshwar Hills is crucial for enhancing educational access and reducing dropout rates. By providing reliable transportation and local educational facilities, the community can support its youth in achieving their educational and professional goals, ultimately contributing to the overall development of the region.

Health Practices

In the remote Male Mahadeshwar Hills region, understanding health is essential for addressing the unique challenges faced by its tribal communities. Health issues in this area are deeply intertwined with geographical, cultural, and infrastructural factors, which collectively shape the well-being of the local population. Studying health in the Male Mahadeshwar Hills region is crucial for several reasons. The unique challenges faced by its tribal communities underscore the need for a comprehensive understanding of their health dynamics. Addressing these challenges can lead to better health outcomes and overall community well-being. The remote location of villages in Male Mahadeshwar Hills presents significant barriers to accessing healthcare. Many residents live far from medical facilities, and the lack of reliable transportation compounds this issue. Studying the impact of geographical isolation on health can inform the development of innovative solutions, such as mobile clinics or telemedicine services, to bridge the gap between healthcare providers and the community. The region is rich in cultural heritage, with traditional healing practices playing a vital role in the community's approach to health. Understanding these practices is essential for integrating them into the broader healthcare framework. This integration can enhance the effectiveness of health interventions by ensuring they are culturally appropriate and respectful of local traditions. Studying these practices also helps preserve valuable indigenous knowledge for future generations.

Similarly, maternal and child health is a critical area of concern in the present time. Issues such as high rates of anaemia among children and emerging health problems among women, like Polycystic Ovary Syndrome (PCOD), require focused attention. Studying these health issues can inform the creation of specialized programs and services that cater to the specific needs of mothers and children, ultimately improving their health outcomes. Further, a thorough understanding of these conditions and their underlying causes can lead to better management strategies. Research can help identify risk factors, improve screening programs, and develop targeted health education initiatives to promote healthier lifestyles and prevent chronic diseases. This approach not only enhances the well-being of the community but also contributes to the preservation of cultural heritage and the overall development of the region. Hence the part of the study focuses on various aspects of health care in Male Mahadeshwara Hills.

Primary Health Centre

Among the surveyed population 71.4 percent reported having access to a nearby Primary Health Centre (PHC), while 28.6 percent stated they did not have access. This indicates that a majority of the population has the benefit of nearby primary healthcare services, facilitating access to essential medical assistance. The notable fact here is that most of the households having access to PHC belong to the nearby villages of MM Hills near the foothill. However, the significant minority without access to a PHC suggests potential gaps in healthcare infrastructure, geographical disparities, hindering healthcare access, and contributing to unequal health outcomes. Ensuring universal access to primary healthcare facilities remains crucial for promoting community health and addressing healthcare needs effectively within Bedagampana.

Availability of Free Medicines

Among the surveyed population 71.4 percent reported having access to free medicines, while 28.6 percent stated they did not. This indicates that a significant portion of the population benefits from the availability of free medicines, potentially through government healthcare programs or other initiatives. However, the proportion of households without access to free medicines highlights potential gaps in healthcare affordability or availability, which impacts healthcare access and health outcomes.

Supply of Sanitary pads in PHCs

Among the surveyed population, 29.5 percent reported that Primary Health Centres (PHCs) supply sanitary pads, while 70.5 percent stated they do not. The PHC also confirmed that there is a provision for the supply of free sanitary pads are there in schools however after COVID it has been stopped. This data suggests that a significant majority of PHCs do not provide sanitary pads, potentially indicating a gap in access to menstrual hygiene products through public health infrastructure. Lack of access to sanitary pads can pose challenges for women and girls in managing menstrual hygiene, potentially impacting their health, dignity, and overall well-being. Addressing this gap by ensuring the availability of sanitary pads in PHCs could contribute to promoting menstrual health and hygiene, empowering women and girls, and reducing barriers to healthcare access.

Support by Anganwadi/ ASHA/ ANM workers

Among the surveyed population 69.5 percent reported receiving support from Anganwadi workers, ASHA (Accredited Social Health Activist) workers, or ANM (Auxiliary Nurse Midwife) workers, while 30.5 percent stated they did not receive such support. This suggests that a majority of households have access to assistance and guidance from these frontline healthcare workers. Support from Anganwadi, ASHA, and ANM workers can play a crucial role in promoting community health, providing essential healthcare services, and offering guidance on various health-related issues, including maternal and child health, nutrition, and disease prevention. However, the proportion of households without access to support from these workers highlights potential gaps in healthcare delivery or outreach efforts, which could impact healthcare access and health outcomes, particularly among vulnerable populations.

Pregnancy and Health Care

Among the surveyed population only 9.5 percent reported having pregnant women at home, while the vast majority, comprising 90.5 percent, stated otherwise. This data suggests a relatively low prevalence of pregnant women within the surveyed households. The presence of pregnant women at home is significant as it may necessitate additional healthcare and support services to ensure the well-being of both the expectant mothers and their unborn children and to understand the demographic composition of the households in the Bedagampana tribal group.

Age of Pregnancy

Among the surveyed households, those reporting a specific age range for pregnancy, 6.7 percent fell within the range of 20–25 years, while 2.8 percent were between 26–30 years old. This data suggests that among households where pregnancy is relevant, a portion of pregnancies occur among women aged 20–30 years old. This data suggests that pregnancies are relatively evenly distributed across these age groups. The optimal age group for pregnancy typically falls between 20 to 35 years due to biological advantages, including healthier eggs and lower risks of complications. The age group generally experiences smoother pregnancies, with better physical and psychological resilience, though individual circumstances and hence it can be said that the people are aware of the age of pregnancy among the Bedagampana tribal group.

Child gap for Pregnancy

Among the surveyed population, 10.5 percent stated a gap of 1–2 years between children, while 3.8 percent reported a gap of 2–3 years, and 1.9 percent reported a gap of 3–5 years. This data suggests varied intervals between childbirths within the surveyed population, with some families opting for shorter or longer intervals between children. Understanding these patterns of child gap durations is essential for family planning programs and analyzing the data it can be observed that the Bedagampana community is scientifically sound about the child gap period as spacing pregnancies around 1–2 years apart is often recommended by health care institutions. This interval allows for maternal recovery, optimal infant care, and reduces health risks associated with closely spaced pregnancies, promoting the well-being of both mother and child.

Pregnancy Complications

Among the surveyed population, only 6.7 percent indicated experiencing such complications. While the majority did not face complications, the presence of complications underscores the importance of maternal healthcare and highlights the need for comprehensive prenatal care to ensure safe pregnancies and childbirth.

Kind Of Delivery Process

Among those reporting specific delivery methods, 33.3 percent percent opted for natural delivery, while 2.9 percent underwent caesarean delivery. This data indicates a preference for natural childbirth among the Bedagampana people, with a small proportion opting for caesarean delivery, likely for medical reasons showcasing the health conditions of Bedagampana women are more likely to get faster recovery and lower risk of complications.

Post- Natal Care Preferred

Among the surveyed population majority opted for hospital-based postnatal care, while 2.9 percent preferred care at home. This data indicates a preference for hospital-based postnatal care, likely due to awareness of medical professionals and facilities.

Person Responsible for Post- Natal Care

Among the surveyed population, 31.4 percent opted for doctors to oversee postnatal care, while 1.0 percent each mentioned elders of the family and ANM (Auxiliary Nurse Midwife). Additionally, 2.9 percent preferred delivery workers for postnatal care. This data underscores the varied preferences for postnatal care providers, with a notable reliance on medical professionals, particularly doctors, for ensuring maternal and infant well-being during the postpartum period. The predominant reliance on doctors for postnatal care aligns with established medical practices, emphasizing the importance of medical oversight during the critical postpartum period. Additionally, the limited mentions of other care providers, such as ANMs, elders of the family, and delivery workers, highlight potential gaps in awareness or access to comprehensive postnatal care services.

Diseases in Last One Year

In the last one year, fever emerges as the most prevalent, affecting both males and females. Diarrhoea follows with a higher incidence among children. Other diseases such as malaria, cholera, chikungunya, rheumatic fever, and anaemia did not register any reported cases within the surveyed population within the last one year. This absence of reported cases indicates either a low prevalence of these diseases within the surveyed population or a lack of diagnosis and reporting. When comparing the prevalence of diseases between males and females, as well as between adults and children, notable differences emerge. Among adults, fever appears to affect both genders fairly evenly, however, among children, there seems to be a slight disparity. In the case of diarrhoea, while there are no reported cases among adult males and females, among children, there's a noticeable discrepancy. This suggests a higher susceptibility of children to diarrhoea within the surveyed population. Overall, these comparisons highlight potential gender and age-based variations in disease susceptibility and underscore the importance of targeted healthcare interventions tailored to specific demographics to address prevalent health concerns effectively.

Preferred Medicine

The overwhelming majority 97.1 percent of respondents indicated a preference for allopathic medicine. This suggests a strong preference or reliance on mainstream medical practices commonly associated with Western medicine, which typically involves the use of pharmaceuticals and surgical interventions. A small percentage 2.9 percent of respondents expressed a preference for local healing systems such as Ayurveda. This indicates a niche preference for traditional or alternative medical practices that are often rooted in cultural and holistic approaches to healthcare. The preference for allopathy reflects broader trends toward modern medical practices, which are often perceived as more standardized and scientifically validated. On the other hand, the minority preference for local healing systems suggests a recognition and value of traditional knowledge and practices in healthcare. Understanding these preferences can inform healthcare policies, medical education, and public health initiatives. It highlights the importance of integrating diverse medical systems to provide comprehensive and culturally sensitive healthcare services.

Case Studies

Two case studies are discussed below to broaden the understanding of healthcare facilities among the villages of Male Mahadeshwar Hills. One case study examines the modern healthcare system, highlighting its infrastructure, accessibility, and the impact it has had on the local population. This includes an analysis of the availability of medical facilities, the qualifications of healthcare professionals, and the community's overall health outcomes. The study also explores the challenges faced by the modern healthcare system, such as limited resources, funding issues, and logistical difficulties in reaching remote areas.

The other case study provides a glimpse into the indigenous and traditional healing system that has been used by Bedagampana for generations. This includes an exploration of traditional healing practices, the role of local healers, and the cultural significance of these methods. The case study also examines how these traditional practices are integrated into the community's daily life and their effectiveness in treating various ailments.

By comparing these two systems, the case studies offer valuable insights into the strengths and limitations of both modern and traditional healthcare practices. This dual approach provides a comprehensive understanding of how both systems coexist and contribute to the overall health and well-being of the Bedagampana community living in the Male Mahadeshwar Hills.

Case Study 1: Primary Health Centre, Male Mahadeshwar Hills

The Primary Health Centre, Male Mahadeshwar Hills is the nearest health centre available for all the villages mentioned in the book. In most of the cases the distance from a village to the Primary Health centre is near about 30 km and no regular transportation services are recorded for emergency cases. The health centre mainly provides day-care services and no admissions are done for emergency cases. In terms of such cases, Tamil Nadu is the most preferred location for the locals for treatment due to its nearer geographical location. Further it is reported that the patients who go to Tamil Nadu are treated with high dosage of medicine causing a quicker relieve for the patients. This is a notable reason for Bedagampana people choosing Tamil Nadu as their preferred health destination.

The average health problems are related with diseases like fluctuation of blood pressure, diabetes, asthma etc. whereas it has been reported by the staff that among children anaemia is a notable disease and almost 15 percent of the reported children are suffered by it. Though sickle cell anaemia has been recorded only in Soliga tribe till now and no patients from Bedagampana are detected under sickle cell yet as the number of diagnostic centres or procedures are negligible hence there is a high probability of sickle cell anaemia among Bedagampana also. Diseases like elephantiasis, leprosy, malaria and other vector borne diseases etc. are not found. The health centre is equipped with general checkup machineries however no major diagnostic facilities like ECG are there. The hospital provides free medicines for diseases like TB and medicines like zinc, iron and folic acid tablets are also provided freely. Some cases of HIV, Cancers (1 or 2 cases) have been diagnosed in the area.

Women related health problems like PCOD are found among the new generation women though no such cases were prevalent among the older generations. Similarly, it has been reported that though the normal delivery is the most common form of childbirth yet in the past 3 to 4 years the cases of caesarean delivery has also been found. It indicates that complications in pregnancy is a very new factor among the local women. Awareness related to women hygiene like use of sanitary pads, and he provision for supply of free sanitary pads are there in schools however after COVID it has been stopped. Cases of birth handicap is found but no cases of Polio are there. The staff further reported that awareness on polio drops, and vaccination are high among the Bedagampana. Even up to February 2024, the hospital staffs like ANM and ASHA workers used to go to each single houses in the villages for vaccination but due to the lack of transport facilities and forest rule the access to forest has become difficult. Hence people come in group from the forest for their general health checkup by themselves.

The health centre consists of one medical officer, two chief health officers, one ANM, five ASHA workers but it is reported that the number of male staff is less, and it is a requirement for them. Two ambulances are there for the convenience of the patients and their family, but the transportation route of the ambulance is limited to the main locality of Male Mahadeshwara as there is no accessible roads available to enter into the villages. From time to time the health centre also conducts awareness programs under SNEHA mission and free medical camps but no such camps are organized in tribal areas of Bedagampana as it is critical to enter into forest areas due to the lack of transportation. During the pandemic time 400 cases of COVID were reported with 12 recorded deaths. The enrolment under Ayushman Card has already been done for all the patients and twelve members out of them have already been confirmed it but none of the patients has taken benefits of it yet.

CHAPTER 5

Case Study 2: Puttanna — The Naati Vaidya (Traditional Healer)

Puttanna is the only naati Vaidya or the traditional healer among the Bedagampana who has been practicing this indigenous knowledge system for last 40 years. He is an expert in curing snake bites and approximately 300 people have been cured by him from snakebites through traditional medicines after which the venom comes out from the mouth of the patients in the form of vomit as reported by him. The people from all nearby 28 to 30 villages comes to him for a cure of different types of diseases. It includes jaundice, piles, mensural cycle problem, tooth and gum problems, etc. for which he uses herbs picked up from the jungle. The duration for relief of general diseases like fever takes 2 days whereas in the case of cough, it goes up to 3 days. As reported by him, the complete cure of snake bite may take sometimes three days. He further stated that he uses grasses like durba (green grass), nagdale plant, etc. as a medicinal herb, and only for the cure of piles he possesses the knowledge of 21 types of medicinal herbs. He has also traditional knowledge of aromatic medicinal plants that can cure migraine or half headaches by smelling the herb seven times though the scientific rationale for this needs to be verified. Other medicinal properties include goat milk for jaundice, breast milk with pinches of turmeric for eye infection, or oldest honey for skin burn, etc. which indicates the use of both flora and fauna as a traditional and ayurvedic healing system.

Puttanna is the only existing Naati Vaidya (traditional healer) among Bedagampana who belong to the Tammadi group of it. He has received all this knowledge system from his past generations and wants to pass it to future generations though he regrets that his upcoming generations are not interested in preserving/ learning this knowledge system. Puttanna is physically disabled and does not charge any fees to cure the needy as he believes in the theory of 'Jeeva dharma' (the religion of living beings). He reported that the jungle is still dense in the nearby areas of the Male Mahadeshwara hills hence none of the medicinal herbs have been destroyed and all of them can be found in the hearts of the forest though there is a need to identify those herbs and to pass the knowledge system scientifically to the upcoming generations. He urges that government assistance can help the traditional knowledge systems of herb and forest products to bring it in scientific and mainstream education.

Summary

Healthcare is a fundamental necessity, and its importance is profoundly evident in the Male Mahadeshwar Hills region, where the tribal population faces significant health challenges. The Primary Health Centre (PHC) in Male Mahadeshwar Hills is the sole healthcare provider for many villages, yet its limitations highlight the critical need for accessible and comprehensive healthcare services. The PHC's role as the primary healthcare provider is crucial due to the geographical isolation of the villages. With distances of around 30 kilometres and lack of regular transportation services, timely access to medical care is severely hindered. This situation emphasizes the importance of having a well-equipped and accessible health centre to address both routine and emergency health needs. The prevalence of chronic conditions such as diabetes, blood pressure fluctuations, and asthma necessitates ongoing medical supervision and management. The PHC provides essential medications and general checkups, but the lack of advanced diagnostic tools limits effective treatment. Improved healthcare infrastructure is vital to manage these conditions and prevent complications. Emerging health issues among women, such as PCOD and increasing cases of caesarean deliveries, indicate changing health dynamics that require specialized care. Moreover, the significant prevalence of anaemia among children underscores the need for nutritional and medical interventions.

Healthcare services play a pivotal role in ensuring maternal and child health through regular checkups, nutritional support, and safe childbirth practices. The absence of diseases like polio and the effective management of TB through free medications illustrate the impact of preventive healthcare measures. However, the presence of diseases such as anaemia and potential undiagnosed cases of sickle cell anaemia highlights the need for comprehensive screening and preventive strategies. Regular health camps and awareness programs are essential for early detection and prevention of diseases. The lack of emergency admissions at the PHC forces residents to seek critical care in Tamil Nadu, often with high medication doses for quick relief. This reliance on external facilities for emergencies underscores the urgent need for local emergency care services. Enhancing the PHC's capabilities to handle emergencies can save lives and reduce the burden of traveling long distances for urgent medical attention. The cessation of sanitary pad distribution post-COVID-19 and the need for ongoing public health initiatives highlight the importance of sustained efforts in promoting hygiene and preventive care. Effective healthcare services can ensure continuous support for hygiene practices and public health education, crucial for preventing health issues related to poor sanitation.

Healthcare in the Male Mahadeshwar Hills region is multifaceted, encompassing both modern medical facilities and traditional healing practices. Puttanna's healing methods highlight a holistic approach, utilizing both flora and fauna in treatments, and are ingrained in the cultural fabric of the Bedagampana community. While the PHC provides structured medical care and essential services, it lacks the personalized, culturally resonant touch that Puttanna's practice offers.

Moreover, Puttanna's work remains largely undocumented and scientifically unverified, posing challenges for integration into mainstream healthcare. Hence, understanding and preserving both modern and traditional health practices is crucial for comprehensive healthcare in the Male Mahadeshwar Hills. Combining these approaches could enhance healthcare delivery, ensuring that both scientific advancements and traditional wisdom contribute to the well-being of the community. Addressing the existing gaps in healthcare accessibility, infrastructure, and services is imperative to improve the health and well-being of the tribal population, ensuring they receive the care and support necessary for a healthier future.

Infrastructure Development

Infrastructure development plays a critical role in fostering the growth and prosperity of communities, serving as the backbone for economic advancement, social well-being, and environmental sustainability. In the context of Male Mahadeshwar Hills, a region endowed with natural beauty and cultural richness, the need for robust infrastructure is particularly pronounced. This section sets the stage to delve into the challenges and opportunities surrounding infrastructure development in this unique and geographically isolated area. Addressing these challenges effectively can pave the way for improved access to essential services, tourism prospects, enhanced livelihoods, and overall community resilience.

Mode of Transportation

The data outlines the modes of transportation utilized within the surveyed community. It reveals that a significant portion, 47.6 percent, relies on their own vehicles for commuting, while an equal percentage, also 47.6 percent, depends on foot as their primary mode of transportation. This significant reliance on walking suggests a potential lack of transportation infrastructure, compelling residents to walk as their primary mode of travel. A small proportion, 4.8 percent, utilizes government buses which are rare to communicate within the villages but are used mainly for traveling to the block areas.

Quality of Transportation Facility

With reference to the preceding section detailing modes of transportation, respondents provided feedback on the quality of transportation facilities. A vast majority, 81.9 percent, rated the quality as 'poor', indicating significant dissatisfaction with the existing transportation infrastructure. Additionally, 18.1 percent described it as 'very poor'. The poor quality of transportation facilities poses a significant concern as it hampers accessibility, mobility, and overall quality of life for residents. Inadequate transportation infrastructure limits opportunities for employment, education, and healthcare, exacerbating socio-economic disparities and hindering community development. Addressing this issue is crucial for fostering inclusivity and prosperity.

Difficulties Due to Poor Transportation

The data underscores the challenges arising from poor transportation infrastructure within the Bedagampana community. A significant majority, 81.0 percent, face difficulties accessing health infrastructure, impacting their ability to receive timely medical care. Additionally, 19.0 percent encounter obstacles in pursuing higher education due to transportation limitations. These difficulties highlight the far-reaching consequences of inadequate transportation, affecting both healthcare access and educational opportunities, and most important lack of job opportunities, thereby compromising residents' well-being and socio-economic advancement.

Basic Water Facility

The data reveals that 73.3 percent of respondents have access to basic water facilities within the surveyed community, while 26.7 percent responded negatively. Access to basic water facilities is essential for ensuring health, sanitation, and overall well-being. However, the sources of water here are mainly based on traditional water resources like wells and some of them have access to bore wells. Though the pipelines have been set up under 'Jal Jeevan Mission' and 'Har Ghar Jal', yet there is no supply of water from these pipelines. Further, the significant portion without access highlights a pressing need to improve water infrastructure to meet the community's urgent needs for *swatch jal* (potable water).

Basic Electricity Facility

The data indicates that 85.7 percent of respondents have access to basic electricity facilities within the surveyed community, while 14.3 percent do not. Access to electricity is crucial for various aspects of daily life, including lighting, cooking, communication, and access to technology. One important factor here is that those who stated in affirmation with the fact of availability of electricity also reported that this electricity is based on solar panels established under Deen Dayal Yojana with four crores invested in each village. However, it has not been beneficial for the villagers as the power is reachable with a break of 15 days to their houses. Most of the time they remain without electricity hence the supply of electricity can be considered in a very poor state. Hence, the data underscores the need to address electricity infrastructure gaps to ensure equitable access for all residents.

Toilet Facility

Among the surveyed population, only 26.7 percent reported having access to toilet facilities, while a significant majority, accounting for 73.3 percent, stated they did not have access. This highlights a substantial gap in access to basic sanitation infrastructure within the surveyed community. Lack of access to toilet facilities can pose significant health risks, including the spread of diseases and hygiene-related issues. It also underscores broader challenges related to infrastructure development, particularly in rural or underserved areas. Addressing the deficit in toilet facilities is crucial for promoting public health, ensuring dignity, and advancing broader development goals related to sanitation and hygiene. Efforts to improve access to sanitation infrastructure should prioritize equitable access for all members of the community, especially vulnerable populations.

Water Facility in Toilet

The table indicates the availability of water facilities in toilets among the sample. Only 26.7 percent reported having access to water facilities in their toilets, while a significant majority of 73.3 percent stated they did not. This glaring lack of access to water in toilet facilities poses severe challenges to hygiene and sanitation standards. Without adequate water facilities, maintaining proper hygiene becomes exceedingly difficult, increasing the risk of diseases and compromising overall health. Moreover, the absence of water in toilets underscores broader issues related to infrastructure development and access to basic amenities, particularly in rural or underserved communities. Addressing this critical deficit in water facilities is imperative for safeguarding public health, promoting dignity, and advancing sustainable development goals related to sanitation and hygiene. Efforts to improve water access in toilets should be prioritized to ensure equitable access for all individuals, thereby enhancing overall well-being and quality of life.

Use of Toilet by All Family Members

The data indicates a significant gap in toilet utilization within households, potentially due to factors such as insufficient toilet facilities. The lack of universal toilet usage within families can pose serious challenges to hygiene and sanitation, increasing the risk of disease transmission and compromising overall health outcomes. It also underscores broader issues related to behavioural practices and awareness regarding the importance of proper sanitation. Addressing barriers to universal toilet usage within households requires comprehensive approaches that include infrastructure improvements, behaviour change interventions, and community engagement initiatives.

Need for Toilet facility

The data underscores the significant demand for improved sanitation infrastructure within the surveyed community. The expressed need for toilet facilities highlights the importance of addressing gaps in sanitation infrastructure to meet the basic needs of individuals and communities. Initiatives aimed at improving access to toilet facilities should prioritize community engagement, infrastructure development, and behaviour change interventions to ensure sustainable and equitable access for all. By meeting the expressed need for toilet facilities, communities can enhance public health, dignity, and quality of life for individuals and families.

Amount Willing to Spend for Toilet

Among the surveyed households, 26.7 percent indicated that the amount they are not willing to spend for a toilet as they have already access to it. However, the majority, accounting for 71.4 percent, were willing to spend between 5000–10000 units of currency for this purpose. A smaller proportion, comprising 1.9 percent, were willing to spend between 2000–5000 units of currency. This data suggests that the majority of individuals prioritize investing a substantial amount in acquiring toilet facilities, indicating a recognition of the importance of sanitation and hygiene. The willingness to allocate funds for toilets underscores the perceived value of such infrastructure in promoting health and well-being within communities. Efforts to improve access to toilets should consider the financial capacity of individuals and aim to provide affordable options that meet their needs and preferences.

Government Policies, Schemes and Benefits

The section illustrates the uptake of various government schemes and benefits within the surveyed community. It examines how effectively these programs are reaching the intended beneficiaries, identifies any barriers to access, and assesses the overall impact on improving the quality of life and economic well-being of the community members.

Availability of Old Age Pension

In the households surveyed, 29.5 percent have access to old age pension, while 70.5 percent do not have access to it. This data underscores a significant portion of the surveyed population lacking this form of financial support during their elderly years. The absence of old age pensions among the majority may indicate potential financial vulnerabilities and limited social safety nets for aging households within the surveyed community. This underscores a need for broader social welfare initiatives to support elderly populations and ensure their financial security in later life.

Widow Pension

The data reveals that out of all of the widows (100 percent) receive a widow pension. This indicates that within the surveyed population, all widows have access to financial support in the form of a pension. This data suggests a positive trend in providing financial assistance to widows, ensuring their economic security following the loss of their spouse. Access to widow pensions is crucial for mitigating financial vulnerabilities and promoting the well-being of widows, allowing them to maintain their livelihoods and independence. This data underscores the importance of social welfare programs in supporting vulnerable populations and highlights the effectiveness of widow pension schemes in providing crucial financial support to those in need.

Assistance to Specially Abled Persons

The data indicates that all of the needy (100 percent) receive assistance for specially abled persons. This suggests that within the surveyed population, all households with disabilities are receiving some form of support or assistance. While the sample size is small, this data portrays a positive trend in providing aid and resources to specially abled households, ensuring their inclusion and access to necessary support services. Accessible assistance is crucial for enhancing the quality of life and promoting the independence of persons with disabilities. This data underscores the importance of inclusive policies and initiatives aimed at addressing the diverse needs of households with disabilities and ensuring their full participation in society.

Further, various other Government initiatives and beneficiaries received by the Bedagampana are as follows:

- PM Jandhan and Aadhar card enjoy universal participation, with 100 percent enrolment.
- Job card registration is relatively low at 23.8 percent, indicating limited engagement in rural employment schemes like MNREGA.
- MNREGA card registration is notably absent, indicating a lack of participation in this rural employment guarantee program.
- Participation in schemes like Document for PAHANI and Ujjwala Scheme is moderate, with 32.4 percent and 86.7 percent enrolment respectively.
- PDS/Ration card enjoys high enrolment at 93.3 percent, indicating widespread access to subsidized food grains. The significant majority of the population

in the sample is categorized under the Antyodaya scheme, which is typically targeted at the poorest households. The Yellow ration card which indicates the people below the poverty line (BPL) is the least prevalent. Overall, the data highlights a predominant reliance on the Antyodaya ration card, reflecting the economic conditions that the targeted surveyed group is in poor economic conditions but the level of households below the poverty line (BPL) is negligible.

- Participation in schemes like Pradhan Mantri Awas Yojana (PMAY) and Swatch Bharat Mission (SBM)/Toilets is absent or minimal, indicating potential gaps in housing and sanitation initiatives.

Overall, the data reflects varying levels of engagement with government schemes and benefits, highlighting the absence of government facilities in most of the cases that address the socio-economic needs within the community.

Reason behind Not Availing Government Schemes/Benefits

In light of the previous part depicting the uptake of various government schemes and benefits, the subsequent data sheds light on the reasons behind the non-availability of these initiatives within the surveyed community. A significant proportion, 82.9 percent, attribute their lack of participation to a dearth of awareness regarding the schemes. This suggests a critical need for enhanced communication and outreach efforts to educate residents about available opportunities. Additionally, 17.1 percent cite non-accessibility by the government, indicating bureaucratic or logistical barriers hindering their ability to access these benefits. These insights underscore the importance of not only expanding awareness but also streamlining processes to ensure equitable access to government support.

Involvement with Self-Help Groups (SHGs)

The data indicates that 19.0 percent of respondents are involved with Self-Help Groups (SHGs), while 81.0 percent are not involved in it. Involvement with SHGs can empower individuals economically and socially through collective action and mutual support. However, the majority not involved suggests potential opportunities for expanding SHG participation to enhance community development and empowerment initiatives, which can also contribute to the income generation of the individuals of the Bedagampana community.

Summary

The data from the survey conducted in Male Mahadeshwar Hills reveals a landscape marked by significant infrastructural deficiencies and critical need for targeted interventions and policy reforms to improve the overall quality of life for residents in this remote area. One of the most pressing issues highlighted in the survey is the inadequate transportation infrastructure. A substantial portion of the population relies on foot as their primary mode of transportation, reflecting the dearth of accessible and reliable transport options. The majority of respondents rated the quality of transportation facilities as poor or very poor, indicating widespread dissatisfaction and significant barriers to mobility. These challenges not only hinder access to essential services such as healthcare and education but also limit economic opportunities, perpetuating socio-economic disparities within the community. Access to basic amenities like water and sanitation also emerges as a critical concern. While a significant portion of respondents reported access to basic water facilities, disparities in water supply from government pipelines remain glaring. Similarly, the lack of access to toilet facilities and water within toilets poses serious hygiene and health risks, underscoring the urgent need for infrastructure improvements. The data reveals varying levels of engagement with government schemes and benefits among the community members. While participation in schemes like PM Jandhan and Aadhar card enrolment is universal, uptake of rural employment schemes like MNREGA, PMAY and Swatch Bharat Mission is notably low. Limited awareness about available schemes emerges as a primary barrier to participation, indicating the need for improved communication and outreach strategies. Involvement with Self-Help Groups (SHGs) is another area where community engagement can foster economic empowerment and social cohesion. Currently, only a small percentage of respondents are involved in SHGs, suggesting untapped potential for collective action and mutual support.

Suggestions and Recommendations

The chapter suggests the following suggestions and recommendations for a better education, health, and infrastructural development.

Improving Transportation Infrastructure

- **Construction of Roads:** Construction of roads connecting villages to educational and healthcare hubs like Male Mahadeshwar Hills can significantly improve accessibility for students and residents.
- **Subsidized Transport Options:** Explore subsidies or incentives for local transport providers to ensure affordable and accessible transport options for residents, particularly students and those in need of healthcare.

Enhancing Educational and Healthcare Access
- **Establish Satellite Educational Centres:** Set up satellite centres for higher education and vocational training within the region to reduce the distance barrier and encourage more students to pursue higher education.
- **Upgrade Healthcare Facilities:** Improve the Primary Health Centre (PHC) in Male Mahadeshwar Hills with advanced diagnostic tools, emergency care capabilities, and specialized services to cater to diverse health needs.

Water and Sanitation Infrastructure
- **Improve Water Supply:** Address disparities in water supply from government pipelines to ensure consistent and safe access to clean water for all residents.
- **Expand Sanitation Facilities:** Invest in building more toilets and ensuring water facilities within them to promote hygiene and prevent health risks associated with poor sanitation.

Enhancing Awareness and Participation in Government Schemes
- **Increase Awareness Campaigns:** Launch targeted awareness campaigns about government schemes like MNREGA, PMAY, and Swatch Bharat Mission to improve participation and uptake among community members.
- **Streamline Application Processes:** Simplify application procedures and providing assistance to residents in completing paperwork for accessing government benefits and services.

Promoting Community Engagement and Empowerment
- **Support Self-Help Groups (SHGs):** Encourage more residents to participate in SHGs by offering training, capacity-building programs, and financial support for income-generating activities.
- **Facilitate Local Initiatives:** Foster partnerships between local communities, NGOs, and government agencies to support grassroots initiatives that address socio-economic challenges and promote community development.

Preserving Traditional and Modern Healthcare Practices
- **Integrate Traditional and Modern Healthcare:** Promote collaborations between traditional healers like Puttanna and modern healthcare providers to combine scientific advancements with culturally resonant healing practices.
- **Document and Validate Traditional Knowledge:** Support efforts to document traditional healing practices scientifically to integrate them into mainstream healthcare systems effectively.

- **Develop Research and Innovations:** Developing research and innovation in indigenous knowledge systems can further help in the documentation of such traditional practices.

Addressing these recommendations requires coordinated efforts from government bodies, local authorities, NGOs, and community stakeholders. By prioritizing infrastructure development, enhancing educational and healthcare access, promoting awareness and participation in government schemes, and fostering community empowerment, Male Mahadeshwar Hills can overcome its current challenges and pave the way for sustainable development and improved quality of life for its residents. These efforts will not only address immediate needs but also contribute to long-term socio-economic growth and resilience in the region.

Vegetarianism and Assertion for Scheduled Tribe Inclusion

Bedagampana as the Only Vegetarian Tribe of India

The Bedagampana tribe, inhabiting the Male Mahadeshwara Hills in Karnataka, stands out in the Indian tribal landscape due to their exclusive adherence to a vegetarian diet. This distinctive characteristic sets them apart from other tribal communities across the country. Whereas other tribes predominantly incorporate non-vegetarian foods into their diets. This concluding section of the study aims to substantiate the claim that the Bedagampana are the only tribe in India with such a unique dietary practice, supported by historical, cultural, and socio-economic references.

The Bedagampana tribe's transition to vegetarianism is intrinsically linked to their historical and cultural evolution. Originally, being a hunting community, the tribe's dietary practices were traditionally non-vegetarian. The pivotal change occurred with various factors like the influence of the ideologies of Veerashaivism and Lingayatism as well as inspired by Swamy Male Mahadeshwara, a revered spiritual leader who transformed the tribe's lifestyle. Historical records and local folk stories emphasize Swamy Male Mahadeshwara's role in this transformation. According to oral traditions and scholarly interpretations, he introduced vegetarianism as a part of a broader religious as well as social reform. This shift was not merely a dietary change but a reflection of deeper spiritual values, integrating the Bedagampana into the Veerashaiva religious tradition, which emphasizes non-violence and purity in food consumption.

EPILOGUE

Comparison with Other Tribal Communities

To substantiate that the Bedagampana are the only vegetarian tribe, it is essential to compare their dietary practices with those of other tribal groups in India. A review of anthropological and ethnographic studies reveals that most Indian tribal communities including the neighbouring Soliga tribes of Male Mahadeshwar hills, include non-vegetarian food in their diets. These communities typically rely on animal products due to their local environments and subsistence needs.

For instance, the Santhals of West Bengal and Jharkhand are known for their consumption of fish and flesh, reflecting their traditional practices and reliance on local resources. Similarly, the Bodos of Assam and the Soligas of Karnataka are documented to include meat in their diets, demonstrating a broader pattern among tribal groups.

Another empirical study done by Harish R P et. al. finds the comparison of Soligas and Bedagampanas dietary practices. As a result, they have shown that Bedagampanas are pure vegetarians and consume wild plants food spices in their daily food consumption.

The Bedagampana's vegetarianism is deeply embedded in their religious practices, which further differentiates them from other tribes. Bedagampana's adherence to vegetarianism is a direct consequence of the religious reforms initiated by Veerashaivas, Lingayats and Swamy Male Mahadeshwara. The Veerashaiva's decree that only vegetarians could perform rituals and offer pooja to the Lord Mahadeshwara established a unique religious dietary practice among the Bedagampana. The integration of vegetarianism into their religious rituals is evidenced by their traditional ceremonies and offerings, which exclusively feature vegetarian foods. This practice is documented in local religious texts and community records, which highlight the community's commitment to non-violence and sanctity in food preparation.

The Bedagampana's strict vegetarianism has significant socio-economic implications. The community's dietary practices have shaped their local economy and interactions with broader market systems. The lack of involvement in the meat trade and related economic activities reflects their unique position within the tribal economic spectrum.

Their dietary practices have also influenced their engagement with external communities and market dynamics. Further, the focus on vegetarianism has created niche economic opportunities, such as promoting vegetarian culinary practices and traditional recipes.

In conclusion, the Bedagampana tribe's status as the only vegetarian tribe in India is substantiated through historical, cultural, and socio-economic lenses.

Their transition from a hunter-gatherer lifestyle to a strict vegetarian diet, influenced by religious reforms, sets them apart from other tribal communities in India. Comparative studies of tribal diets, religious influences, and socio-economic impacts reinforce their unique position in the Indian tribal context. This singular dietary practice not only highlights the Bedagampana's distinctive cultural identity but also reflects broader themes of religious influence, cultural preservation, and socio-economic adaptation. The evidence supports the claim that the Bedagampana are indeed a unique example of vegetarianism within India's diverse tribal landscape.

The Case for Granting Scheduled Tribe Status to the Bedagampana Community

The Bedagampana community, with its rich history and cultural heritage, presents a compelling case for being recognized as a Scheduled Tribe (ST) in India. Despite their deep roots and tribal characteristics, they have been overlooked in the official lists, leading to socio-economic disadvantages.

1. Historical Validation:

The Bedagampana community has a documented history spanning over 600 years, with inscriptions and oral traditions confirming their tribal roots. The Bedagampana community's existence is well-documented through various historical inscriptions such as Haradanalli Shasana, Haidarali Shasana, and Veera Ballala Shasana. Their history spanning over before the arrival of Basaveshwara, the 'Father of Lingayatism' not only validates their long-standing presence but also highlights their traditional roles and contributions to the region's history. The name 'Bedagampana' itself is indicative of their tribal roots, with 'Beda' referring to hunters, 'Gam' indicating tribal affiliation, and 'Pana' meaning community. This nomenclature aligns them with other recognized tribal groups such as Beda, Berad, or Bedara, who are already listed in the Indian Scheduled Tribes list.

2. Geographical Isolation:

The Bedagampana community resides in the remote Male Mahadeshwara Hills, a region characterized by its difficult terrain and limited accessibility. This geographical isolation has significantly contributed to their socio-economic backwardness. The lack of basic amenities such as electricity, water, and transportation exacerbate their living conditions, making it challenging for them to access healthcare, education, and employment opportunities.

The community's livelihood primarily depends on agriculture and forest-based activities, which are often disrupted by environmental and policy changes. The recent ban on cattle rearing in forest areas, for instance, has severely impacted their dairy farming practices, further destabilizing their economic foundation.

3. Cultural Distinctiveness:

The Bedagampana community's transformation under the influence of Swamy Male Mahadeshwara is a significant aspect of their cultural history. Swamy Male Mahadeshwara, a revered figure, played a crucial role in integrating the Bedagampana into the broader Veerashaiva culture. Despite these changes, the Bedagampana maintained their distinct identity.

The Bedagampana community exhibits distinct cultural traits that differentiate them from the broader Veerashaiva Lingayat community with which they have been historically merged. Their traditional practices, such as burying the dead, giving Vadhu Dakshina in marriages, and widow remarriage, naming and pregnancy rituals, nature-worship rituals, traditional medicinal practices, and distinctive customs, which align with tribal characteristics.

4. Lack of Recognition:

Despite their clear tribal characteristics, the Bedagampana community has not been recognized as a Scheduled Tribe, leading to a significant identity crisis. This lack of recognition has deprived them of various government benefits and schemes designed for tribal communities, such as the PM JANMAN Yojana and access to ashram schools. Their inclusion in the Veerashaiva Lingayat category (Category III (B) of the backward community list) is based on their adoption of certain Veerashaiva practices, primarily for religious reasons. However, this classification fails to account for their distinct tribal identity and socio-economic challenges. The conflation of their tribal identity with the Veerashaiva Lingayat community has resulted in a denial of their rightful place in the Scheduled Tribe list.

5. Socio-Economic Backwardness:

The Bedagampana community experiences severe socio-economic challenges, including limited access to healthcare, education, and employment, exacerbated by their geographical isolation.

6. Government Commission Reports and Recommendations:

Several government commissions and reports have highlighted the need for a nuanced understanding of tribal identity and the criteria for ST status. The Lokur Committee (1965) and Dhebar Commission (1960–61) established criteria based on primitive traits, distinct culture, geographical isolation, and socio-economic backwardness. The Kunwar Committee (2006) emphasized the need for recognizing communities suffering from extreme social, educational, and economic backwardness due to geographical isolation. The Bhuria Committee (2002–2004) and the Virginius Xaxa report (2014) further elaborated on the criteria for defining tribes. The Xaxa Committee, in particular, emphasized the importance of historical and political contexts in understanding tribal identities. The recent Task Force led by Hrusikesh Panda (2014) also formulated new criteria, including socio-economic backwardness, geographical isolation, distinct language/dialect, and cultural practices. Based on the established criteria and the specific context of the Bedagampana community, several points justify their inclusion in the Scheduled Tribe list and provide a framework that supports the recognition of the Bedagampana community as a Scheduled Tribe.

Potential Benefits and Implications of Recognition

Recognition of the Bedagampana community as a Scheduled Tribe (ST) can have far-reaching benefits and implications, enhancing their socio-economic status and preserving their cultural heritage. Below, the book outlines several key areas where this recognition can bring substantial changes.

1. Access to Government Schemes and Benefits:

One of the primary advantages of being recognized as a Scheduled Tribe is access to numerous government welfare schemes. These schemes cover a wide range of areas including education, healthcare, housing, and employment. For instance, ST students are eligible for scholarships, free or subsidized education, and residential schools which can significantly improve literacy and educational attainment in the community. Healthcare benefits, including free medical camps and improved access to primary health centres, can address prevalent health issues like anaemia and potential sickle cell disease.

2. Economic Development and Employment Opportunities:

Economic upliftment is another critical area where ST recognition can make a difference. Various government initiatives provide job reservations in public sector employment, financial assistance for starting businesses, and skill development programs. This can help reduce poverty levels, create sustainable livelihoods, and integrate the Bedagampana into the broader economic framework of the country. Additionally, access to microfinance and entrepreneurship development programs can empower community members, particularly women, fostering economic independence and growth.

3. Protection of Land and Forest Rights:

As a recognized ST, the Bedagampana community would be entitled to individual and community rights over forest land under the Forest Rights Act (2006). This includes the right to live on forest land, the right to cultivate land, and the right to use and manage forest resources. Such rights can secure their traditional livelihoods, prevent displacement, and promote sustainable management of forest ecosystems.

4. Preservation of Cultural Heritage:

Recognition can also play a crucial role in preserving and promoting the cultural heritage of the Bedagampana. Government recognition often comes with support for cultural programs, festivals, and the documentation of oral histories and traditions. This not only helps in preserving the unique identity of the tribe but also instills a sense of pride and belonging among the community members. Additionally, such initiatives can raise awareness and appreciation of the tribe's cultural contributions among the broader population.

5. Political Representation and Empowerment:

Scheduled Tribe recognition can empower the Bedagampana community by giving them a voice in decision-making processes through political representation that affect their lives. It can lead to more inclusive policies and programs tailored to their specific needs and challenges, thereby fostering greater social and political integration.

6. Improved Infrastructure and Basic Amenities:

Recognition as Scheduled tribe facilitates government investment in infrastructure development within the Bedagampana settlements. This includes improved access to clean drinking water, sanitation, electricity, and transportation. Enhanced infrastructure not only improves the quality of life but also connects the community to broader economic opportunities and services.

7. Social Equity and Justice:

Finally, ST recognition is a step towards achieving social equity and justice. It acknowledges the historical injustices and marginalization faced by the Bedagampana community. By providing them with the necessary legal and social safeguards, the recognition can promote equality, reduce discrimination, and ensure that the community has equal opportunities to participate in the socio-economic development of the nation.

In conclusion, recognizing the Bedagampana community as a Scheduled Tribe is not merely an administrative formality; it is a dynamic step that can empower the community, enhance their quality of life, and preserve their unique cultural identity. By addressing their socio-economic, political, and cultural needs comprehensively, such recognition can pave the way for a more inclusive and equitable society.

Recommendations and Suggestions

The Bedagampana tribe, with its unique status as the only exclusively vegetarian tribe in India, represents a compelling case for the recognition of Scheduled Tribe (ST) status. Based on the detailed examination of their historical, cultural, socio-economic, and political dimensions, the following recommendations and suggestions are proposed.

1. Formal Recognition as a Scheduled Tribe

Recommendation: The Bedagampana community should be formally recognized as a Scheduled Tribe under the Indian Constitution.

Rationale: Historical records and cultural practices clearly indicate the Bedagampana's tribal roots and their distinct identity. Despite their significant cultural and socio-economic challenges, they have been excluded from the Scheduled Tribe list. Recognition would address this disparity, providing them with the benefits and protections that are afforded to other tribal communities.

Action Steps:

- The relevant state and central government authorities should initiate the process for formal inclusion of the Bedagampana in the Scheduled Tribe list.
- A dedicated committee should be established to discuss the tribe's requirements based on historical, cultural, and socio-economic criteria.

2. Enhancing Socio-Economic Support

Recommendation: Implement targeted socio-economic support programs for the Bedagampana community.

Rationale: The community faces severe socio-economic disadvantages, including limited access to education, healthcare, employment and especially lack of transport facilities. Formal ST recognition would enable access to government schemes specifically designed for tribal communities.

> **Action Steps:**
> - Develop and implement educational support programs, including scholarships and residential schools tailored to the needs of Bedagampana children.
> - Provide healthcare initiatives such as mobile health clinics and subsidized medical services to address prevalent health issues.
> - Introduce economic development programs including job reservations, skill development, and microfinance opportunities.
> - Provide road infrastructure for the people living in the heart of the Male Mahadeshwar Hills.

3. Preservation and Promotion of Cultural Heritage

Recommendation: Support initiatives aimed at preserving and promoting the Bedagampana's unique cultural heritage.

Rationale: The Bedagampana's cultural practices and dietary customs are integral to their identity. Recognizing their unique cultural heritage can foster pride and cultural continuity.

> **Action Steps:**
> - Fund cultural preservation projects such as documentation of oral histories, traditional practices, and festivals.
> - Promote cultural tourism by developing initiatives that showcase Bedagampana traditions, enhancing their visibility and fostering economic opportunities through tourism.

4. Infrastructure Development

Recommendation: Invest in infrastructure development within Bedagampana settlements.

Rationale: Improved infrastructure is crucial for enhancing the quality of life and connecting the community to broader economic and social opportunities.

Action Steps:

- Prioritize investments in basic amenities such as clean drinking water, sanitation, electricity.
- Develop and upgrade road facilities in the region to improve access to essential services.

5. Political Representation and Empowerment

Recommendation: Ensure political representation and empowerment for the Bedagampana community.

Rationale: Political representation can amplify the community's voice in decision-making processes and ensure that their specific needs are addressed.

Action Steps:

- Reserve seats for Bedagampana representatives in local panchayats and state legislatures.
- Provide training and capacity-building programs for community members to enhance their political participation and advocacy skills.

6. Monitoring and Evaluation

Recommendation: Establish a monitoring and evaluation framework to assess the impact of ST recognition and related initiatives.

Rationale: Continuous assessment will ensure that the benefits of ST recognition and support programs are effectively implemented and adapted to meet the community's evolving needs.

Action Steps:

- Create an independent body to monitor the implementation of ST recognition benefits and report on their impact.
- Conduct regular evaluations of socio-economic programs, infrastructure projects, and cultural initiatives to ensure effectiveness and accountability.

7. Inter-Governmental and Community Collaboration

Recommendation: Foster collaboration between government bodies, non-governmental organizations (NGOs), and the Bedagampana community.

Rationale: Collaboration can enhance the effectiveness of support programs and ensure that they are aligned with the community's needs and priorities.

Action Steps:

- Facilitate partnerships between state and central government agencies, Mutts, NGOs, and the Bedagampana community to coordinate support efforts.
- Engage the community in the planning and implementation of development projects to ensure that initiatives are culturally appropriate and sustainable and as per their needs.

Conclusion

The recognition of the Bedagampana as a Scheduled Tribe presents a transformative opportunity to address historical injustices, enhance socio-economic development, and preserve their unique cultural heritage. By implementing these recommendations, the government can support the Bedagampana community in overcoming socio-economic barriers, promote and ensure a more inclusive and equitable society. Inclusion of Bedagampana in Scheduled tribe list will also give them a cultural identity and officially recognize them as 'the first and only vegetarian tribe of India.'

Bibliography

1. 'Create Bedagampana community and include in Schedule Tribes list', *The Hindu*, April 5, 2021.
2. Chaudhari, C. C.: "The coming of the Devi: Adivasi assertion in South Gujarat (Western India)", *International Journal of Research in all Subjects in Multi Languages*, 6(3), 27, 2018.
3. Draft National Tribal Policy, Ministry of Tribal Affairs, Government of India, 2006.
4. Thurston E. and Rangachari K.: *Castes and Tribes of Southern India*, Vol.7 T – Z, Government Press, Madras, 1909.
5. First Backward Classes Commission Report by Kaka Kalelkar, Volume-II, Government of India, 1955
6. Buchanan, F.: *A Journey from Madras through the countries of Mysore, Canara, and Malbar*, 1807, 2011 & 2012, Cambridge University Press.
7. Geethanjali T M: "Folk Legend Malai Mahadeshwara – A Cultural Study", *Indian Journal of Multilingual Research and Development*, Vol.2, Issue.2, 2021.
8. Hardiman, D.: *The Coming of the Devi: Adivasi Assertion in Western India*, Oxford University Press, Delhi, 1987.
9. Harisha R.P., Padmavathy S.: Knowledge and Use of Wild Edible Plants in Two Communities in Malai Mahadeshwara Hills, Southern India, *International Journal of Botany*, Vol.9, Issue.2, 2013.
10. Harisha R.P., Gowthami R., and Siddappa Setty R.: "Vocal to local: Indigenous dietary Practices And Diversity Of Wild Food Plants In Malai Mahadeshwara Wildlife Sanctuary, South India", *A Journal of Plants, People, and Applied Research, Ethnobotany Research, and Applications*, 2021, www.ethnobotany-journal.org
11. Harisha R.P., Gowthami R., and Siddappa Setty R.: "Understanding the Phyllanthus And Terminalia Chebula Species Population Change, Dependency And Sustainability: A Study In Malai Mahadeshwara Hills Wildlife Sanctuary, Southern India", *International Journal of Environment*, ISSN 2091-2854, Volume-12, Issue-1, 2023.
12. Havanur L. G.: Karnataka Backward Classes Commission Report (constituted under the Commissions of Inquiry Act, 1952, Central Act 60 of 1952), Government of Karnataka, Vol.1, Part I, 1975.
13. Hunsal S. M.: *The Lingayat Movement*, Basava Samiti, Bangalore 2004. Print

14. Jyothi, H.P.: "A study on Livelihood Opportunities among the Bedagampana Tribe in Hanur Taluk, Chamarajanagara District of Karnataka State", *International Research Journal of Management Sociology and Humanities*, Vol.11, Issue.1, 2020.

15. Karnataka State Gazatter – Mysore -1988.

16. Kavitha, N.: "Social Life of Bedakampana Lingayats Living in Thalakkarai Hamlet of Anthiyur Taluk in Erode District", *International Journal of Research in Humanities and Social Sciences*, Vol. 4. Issue. 2, 2017.

17. Kontham, S.: "Economic conditions of the Bedagampana community in Chamarajanagar district in Karnataka and Erode district in Tamil Nadu", *International Journal of Enhanced Research in Management & Computer Applications*, vol.6, Issue.3, 2017.

18. Keshavan Prasad, K.: *Male Madeshwara: A Kannada Oral Epic as Sung by Hebbani Madayya and His Troupe*, translated by C. N. Ramachandran, L. N. Bhat. Sahitya Akademi, New Delhi. 2001.

19. Munavalli, S. Lingayat Dharma (Veerashaiva Religion). 2007. https://vsna-public.s3.amazonaws.com/publications/Publication_Lingayat_Dharma.pdf. Accessed on 21.10.2024.

20. Prajavani – News Paper, June 25, 2022.

21. Premapallavi C B: Maya's Beda Budakattina Aaradhya Daivagalu - Samasrutiya Adhyayana, Karnataka Sahithya Academy, Bangalore, 2019.

22. Ramakrishnappa, D.C.: "Oral epics of Male Mahadeshwara: Women and Society", *International Journal of Academic Research*, Vol.9, Issue.1, January 2022.

23. Rangaswamy H: "Myths of Malai Mahadeshwara in connection to Soliga's Tribal Community", *Indian Scholar* (An International Multidisciplinary Research e-journal), Vol.3, Issue.II, 2016.

24. Report of the Excluded and Partially Excluded Areas (Other than Assam) Sub-Committee by A.V. Thakkar, Government of India, 1947.

25. Report of the Scheduled Areas and Scheduled Tribes Commission, by UN Dhebar, Government of India, 1960–1961

26. Report of the Advisory Committee on the Revision of the Lists of Scheduled Castes and Scheduled tribes. by B. N. Lokur, Department of Social Security, Government of India, 1965.

27. Report of the Scheduled Areas and Scheduled Tribes Commission by Dileep Singh Bhuria, Government of India, 2004

28. Report of National Commission for Scheduled Tribes by Kunwar Singh, Government of India, 2006

29. Report of the High Level Committee on Socioeconomic, Health and Educational Status Of Tribal Communities Of India by V. Xaxa, Ministry Of Tribal Affairs, Government Of India, May 2014
30. Singh, K.S.: *The Scheduled Tribes*. New Delhi: Anthropological Survey of India. 1997.
31. "Tamil Nadu government urged to create new Bedgampana community", The Hindu, March 01, 2022.
32. Tietenberg, Tom, 2003, Environmental and Natural Resource Economics, Pearson Education, Delhi. 1909.
33. "Tribals who perform puja to Lord Mahadeshwara will be relocated", The Times of India, June 29, 2020.
34. Vidyarthi, L.P. and B.K. Rai: *The Tribal Culture of India*. New Delhi: Concept Publishing Company. 1985.
35. Xaxa, V.: *State, Society and Tribes: Issues in Post-colonial India*, New Delhi: Pearson. 2008.

Index

Bhuria Committee 50, 85

Case Studies 59–61, 68–70
Category III (B) 47–8, 53, 84
Clans and Sub-groups 23
Cultural Expressions 36–8

Dietary Practices 8–9, 25, 32–3, 44–5, 60, 81–82
Dhebar Commission 49, 84

Education, 56–61
Economy and Occupations 30–2
Electrical Facility 73

Family, Land, and Living Conditions 26–9
Folk Songs 13, 19, 20, 23

Government Policies, Schemes, and Benefits 75–7

Health Practices 63–70, 72
Holy Man 24
Hunters 24, 83

Indo-Western Concepts of Tribe 50

Jangama 12, 14–5, 18

Kaka Kalelkar Commission 51
Karayya and Billayya 18, 20–21, 48
Kunwar committee 50, 85

Lingayatism
    Theologies 2–4, 47, 52, 81, 83
    Lingayat Movement, influence 3, 2–4, 13, 47
Lingadharana 15, 44, 45, 52
Lokur Committee 49, 84

Male Mahadeshwara, Hill Ranges 18

Marriage Practice 40–1, 42
Mutt Cultures, influence 18, 22, 45

Naati Vaidya, 70
Neelayya – Sankamma 20, 37

Oralities 6, 11, 20–1, 43–4, 48
Origin and History 12

Panchacharya 13-5
Pastoral Communities 16-7
Primary Health Centre 53, 64, 68–70, 79, 85

Religion and Spirituality 35, 42–4
Rituals and Traditions 4, 35, 38–42

Sacred Bull 14–6
Salur Mutt 15, 22, 45, 60–1
Sharana Samskruthi 19, 21, 47
Scheduled Tribe, Assertion in 83–90
Swamy Male Mahadeshwara 11–2, 19–23, 41, 81–4

Tammadi 14, 16–7, 23, 26, 39–40, 44, 59, 70
Task Force Panda, Hrusikesh 51, 85
Toilet Infrastructure 56, 59–61, 74–5
Totems 17–8, 38
Transportation 72–3
Tribal Communities
    Budgajangamaru 13–4
    Myasa Beda 16–8
    Soliga 45–9

Veerashaiva, Religious Rites 15, 18, 44, 53
Vegetarianism vii, 1, 12–3, 16, 20, 22, 25, 32–4, 44, 46, 81, 82–3

Water Facility 61, 73–4

Xaxa Committee 50–1, 85

Printed by
CPI books GmbH, Leck